Charles William Stubbs

Christus Imperator

A series of lecture-sermons on the universal empire of Christianity

Charles William Stubbs

Christus Imperator

A series of lecture-sermons on the universal empire of Christianity

ISBN/EAN: 9783337309794

Printed in Europe, USA, Canada, Australia, Japan

Cover: Foto ©Lupo / pixelio.de

More available books at **www.hansebooks.com**

CHRISTUS IMPERATOR

A SERIES OF LECTURE-SERMONS ON

THE UNIVERSAL EMPIRE OF CHRISTIANITY

EDITED BY

CHARLES WILLIAM STUBBS, D.D.

DEAN OF ELY

Regnum tuum, Domine, regnum omnium sæculorum: et dominatio tua in omni generatione et generationem

LONDON

MACMILLAN AND CO.

AND NEW YORK

1894

DEDICATION

TO MY LATE PARISHIONERS AT WAVERTREE

My dear People,—The series of Lecture-Sermons in the present volume was delivered, as you know, in S. Bridget's Church—the Chapel-of-Ease to our Parish Church of Wavertree—on the Sunday Evenings of the Advent Season of 1893. The Lectures are now published, partly in fulfilment of a promise made by me not only to many of you who heard them delivered at S. Bridget's, but to many also in the wider neighbourhood of the city who read them when printed afterwards in the pages of *The Liverpool Pulpit*. They are published, also, partly that through them I at least may be reminded, in hours possibly of despondency or of failure, of the buoyant hopes, the uplifting emotions, the active sympathy which must ever be associated in my mind with memories of happy work and worship in Liverpool. For six years now, as the great Church seasons have come round, it has been my duty and my pleasure to organise for you, either in Wavertree Parish Church or in S. Bridget's, similar groups of Sermon-Lectures. By this means I am glad to think I have been able to give you the opportunity of hearing many of the most distinguished leaders of thought in the Church of to-day. Indeed, the pulpit of S. Bridget's—I think I am making no undue boast—has done much during the last year or two to vindicate in Liverpool the comprehensiveness and catholicity, no less than the devotion and sound learning, of our national Church. For as we have heard in S. Bridget's men of all parties, so we have discussed subjects of all kinds. There has been but one limitation: that the teachers have spoken and the message has been delivered under the solemn sense of the invocation with which each Lecture or Sermon has begun: 'In the name of the Father, and of the Son, and of the Holy Ghost. Amen!'

The general purpose which underlies the Lectures of the present volume has in reality been the aim of any message I have ever had to give you during my ministry in Liverpool. I have desired always to make you feel how the Lord Jesus Christ claims supremacy over all human realms of thought and action, and how that claim ought to affect and influence the moral character no less than the intellectual attitude of every one of His baptized disciples. As a pledge at least of that purpose—all too feebly pursued—as a memento of grateful affection—all too generously reciprocated—will you accept from me as a farewell gift the dedication of this book?

CHARLES W. STUBBS.

DEANERY, ELY,
  September 3, 1894.

LIST OF SUBJECTS AND AUTHORS

		PAGE
I.	THE SUPREMACY OF CHRIST IN ALL REALMS,	1
	By the Very Rev. CHARLES STUBBS, D.D., Dean of Ely.	
II.	CHRIST IN THE REALM OF HISTORY,	18
	By the Very Rev. G. W. KITCHIN, D.D., Dean of Winchester.	
III.	CHRIST IN THE REALM OF PHILOSOPHY,	36
	By the Rev. R. E. BARTLETT, M.A., Bampton Lecturer 1888.	
IV.	CHRIST IN THE REALM OF LAW,	54
	By the Rev. J. B. HEARD, M.A., Hulsean Lecturer 1893.	
V.	CHRIST IN THE REALM OF ART,	73
	By the Rev. Canon RAWNSLEY, M.A., Vicar of Crosthwaite.	
VI.	CHRIST IN THE REALM OF ETHICS,	108
	By the Rev. J. LLEWELYN DAVIES, D.D., Vicar of Kirkby Lonsdale, and Chaplain to the Queen.	
VII.	CHRIST IN THE REALM OF POLITICS,	135
	By the Rev. and Hon. W. H. FREMANTLE, M.A., Canon of Canterbury.	
VIII.	CHRIST IN THE REALM OF SCIENCE,	151
	By the Rev. BROOKE LAMBERT, B.C.L., Vicar of Greenwich.	
IX.	CHRIST IN THE REALM OF SOCIOLOGY,	176
	By the Rev. S. A. BARNETT, M.A., Warden of Toynbee Hall, and Canon of Bristol.	
X.	CHRIST IN THE REALM OF POETRY,	189
	By the Very Rev. CHARLES STUBBS, D.D., Dean of Ely.	

THE SUPREMACY OF CHRIST IN ALL REALMS

'*All things have been created through Him and unto Him, and He is before all things, and in Him all things hold together: and He is the Head of the body, the Church, that in all things He might have the pre-eminence.*'—COL. i. 16, 17, 18.

IN one of the grandest works of the world's literature, Socrates is described by Plato as gradually building up for his disciples the conception of a perfect kingdom, hardly to be realised, he fears, on earth, but of which he thinks perhaps there is a pattern laid up somewhere in the heavens, in which kings are to be philosophers and philosophers kings. In that magnificent vision he pictures for his disciples a state in which wisdom and temperance and justice are to reign supreme, and in which each citizen is to devote himself chiefly to the perfecting of his own moral character. 'He will not, then,' breaks in one disciple very shrewdly, 'he will not, then, of course, engage in

Politics?' 'No, Glaucon,' replies Socrates, 'certainly not—unless some Divine event befall!'

'*Unless some Divine event befall!*' My friends, it is because we believe that that Divine event, for which the great Greek teacher wistfully and vaguely seemed to hope, has come to pass, that you and I are gathered together in this building to-night: it is, at any rate, because I believe that that Divine event has befallen, that I shall not hesitate to ask you, in this place of worship and of prayer, in this series of Lecture-Sermons which we are now commencing, not only to engage in Politics, to think earnestly about Politics, but also about Art and Poetry and Science, and Philosophy and Law and Ethics, and Sociology and all other realms of human thought and activity: it is because I believe that that Divine event has befallen that I have, I think, a right also to ask you that you should recognise that the Christian conquest of all these realms is necessary to the completion of that ideal society for which we daily pray when we say 'Thy kingdom come on earth,' and over which, we believe, the Imperial Christ must one day reign supreme.

In 'that Divine event' you and I have already publicly in this church to-day expressed our belief, when we took the words of the universal Christian Creed upon our lips: 'I believe in one Lord Jesus

Christ, the only begotten Son of God . . . by whom all things were made, who for us men and for our salvation came down from heaven, and was made man.'

What exactly do we mean by these words?

Do we mean what St. Paul meant when, writing to the Colossian Church, he used the words which I read as my text?

Let me remind you of the whole passage. It is, with the parallel argument in the letter to the Ephesian Church, one of the most important passages doctrinally in the whole of the New Testament. I will read it from the revised version:

'He is the image of the invisible God, the firstborn of all creation: for in Him were all things created, in the heavens and upon the earth, things visible and things invisible, whether thrones, or dominions, or principalities, or powers: all things have been created through Him and unto Him: and He is before all things, and in Him all things hold together: and He is the head of the body, the Church: who is the beginning, the firstborn from the dead; that in all things He might have the pre-eminence. For it was the good pleasure (of the Father) that in Him should all the Fulness dwell: and through Him to reconcile all things to Himself, having made peace through the blood of the cross: through Him (I say) whether things upon the earth or things in the heavens.'

The companion passage in the Ephesians speaks of 'the Dispensation of the fulness of the times in which Christ is to sum up all things in the heavens and the things upon the earth. . . . And to be far above all rule and authority and power and dominion, and every name that is named not only in this age, but also in that which is to come. And He put all things in subjection under His feet, and gave Him to be Head over all things to the Church, which is His body, the Fulness of Him that filleth all in all.'

It is not necessary now that I should enter carefully into the exact meaning of the various phrases of these passages, for in the third Lecture of the course, when we come to deal with the relation of Philosophy and Christianity, it will probably be necessary for the lecturer to return to them, in discussing the influence of Greek thought in the development of the early Christian Creeds. But you must not suppose that the various words and phrases of the passage which I have just read to you are as redundant in the Greek as they appear to be to our ears in the English. The whole argument is in reality most concise and condensed, and in every word of it must have carried to the original hearers the thought of some of the deepest subjects of philosophic speculation about which the human mind can be busied.

It is sufficient for us now and here to say this. You have probably in this passage of St. Paul the earliest authoritative record of the Apostolic teaching with regard to the Personality of Christ.

That doctrine I may broadly state thus:—

The Christian Creed announces to us not in the first place a world-wide Philosophy, or even a universal Religion, but it introduces us to a Supreme Person—Jesus Christ, our Lord. In heaven as on earth, over things invisible as over things visible, over things immaterial as over things material, this Person is represented as Supreme.

In the natural creation, in the Universe, His supremacy is that of the Eternal Reason, the pre-incarnate Word of God, the Logos of Greek thought, by whose agency the world of matter was created and is sustained, who is at once the beginning and the end of material things. 'All things have been created through Him and unto Him.'

And in the spiritual creation, in the Church, this same Person is represented as the inspirer and the illuminator of man in his intellectual being, the light and the life of humanity, the revealer to man of the

Divine character, 'manifesting God with increasing clearness at each successive stage in the great scale of being,' until, in the fulness of time, He Himself 'for us men and for our salvation came down from heaven, and . . . was incarnate, . . . and was made man.'

This doctrine of the Incarnation of the Christ implies the exaltation of human nature, and the consecration of all human relations with the visible creation, and, in connection with the conquest of sin and death, opens up the vista of the glorious destiny of the children of God, purposed before the world was.

Now, this doctrine of the Pre-incarnate Word and the Incarnate Christ, though it undoubtedly stands in the forefront of the prologue to St. John's Gospel, though it is hardly less prominent in the opening to the Epistle to the Hebrews, and though it finds special emphasis in the two great Christological passages which I have quoted from the Epistles to the Ephesians and the Colossians, and though lastly it forms the groundwork of the great Creed which is common to all the Churches, in reality, until lately, has exercised very little influence over modern thought.

The loss is most serious. 'How much'—says the late Bishop Lightfoot in commenting on this Epistle —'our theological conceptions suffer in breadth and fulness by this neglect a moment's reflection will show. How much more hearty would be the sympathy of theologians with the revelations of science and the developments of history, if they habitually connected them with the operation of the same Divine Word who is the centre of all their religious aspirations, it is needless to say. Through the recognition of this idea with all the consequences which flow from it as a living influence, more than in any other way, may we hope to strike the chords of that " vaster music " which results only from the harmony of knowledge and faith, of reverence and research.'[1]

It is because I have for long felt the truth of this opinion of Bishop Lightfoot, and because I know from the personal experience of my own early theological training here in Liverpool, how in this city, for more than two generations at any rate, the leaders of Church thought have preached to us for the most part a narrow individualistic Gospel, reaching hardly ever beyond mere theories of personal atonement and schemes of individual salvation, so narrow as to be but a travesty of the true Apostolic, Evangelical, Catholic truth, that I have desired, if possible, to give you and others of my fellow-citizens the opportunity of hearing, from the lips of Churchmen, who are

[1] Lightfoot's *Colossians*, p. 116.

acknowledged leaders in English theology, the announcement of a Gospel which will pass behind the pinched and narrow faith of the Augustinian theology to the richer, more large-hearted, more inspiring Doctrine of the Incarnation, which is characteristic of the great Greek Christian Fathers of the early Church, Clement of Alexandria, Origen, Hippolytus: of the Oxford Reformers, in the fifteenth century, those children of the Revival of Learning, Colet, Erasmus, and More; of the Cambridge Platonists of the seventeenth century, Benjamin Whichcot, John Smith, Dr. Cudworth; with all of whom the broader theologians of our own day, Lightfoot, Frederick Maurice, Westcott, at Cambridge, Dean Stanley, Dr. Hatch, Dr. Jowett, at Oxford, may claim direct affinity.

It will be the object, I know, of those Lecturers who are to follow me in this place to take the Doctrine of the Incarnation, of the Pre-incarnate Word, and the Incarnate Christ as the basis of all their teaching. Starting from that fundamental doctrine of the Christian Creed, it will be their endeavour to show how and why the Lord Jesus Christ claims Supremacy over all realms of human thought and action, and how and why that claim ought to affect and influence the moral character no less than the intellectual attitude of every baptized disciple of Jesus.

It may perhaps help you to grasp the general design of the whole argument, if I now rapidly indicate what appears to me to be the special relation of the fundamental doctrine of Christ's Supremacy to the various subjects named in the sub-titles of the Lectures which are to follow.

What then in the light, on the one hand of Evolution, and on the other of the Incarnation, is meant by the Supremacy of Christ in History?

It means, in the first place, that God has a plan for the world: it means that Order and Progress in Human civilisation is real: it means that the cry of the cynic and the social agnostic—

> 'Fill the can and fill the cup:
> All the windy ways of men
> Are but dust that rises up,
> And is lightly laid again.
>
> Drink to lofty hopes that cool—
> Visions of a Perfect State:
> Drink we last the Public fool,
> Frantic love and frantic hate'—

is not only not true, but is a gross blasphemy against God's purpose for Humanity: it means that God has for the world a great educational plan by which both the perfection of the individual and the perfection of the race is to be accomplished: it means that, in the development of that plan, each age of the world has its own special work to do: it means that Progress is not only a vital fact of human existence, but that it is its vital law: it means that there *is* a Christian ideal for Society, that there *is* a Social Order which is the best, and that towards this Order the world is gradually moving: and finally it means that Christ, as the Eternal Word of God, has always been and is still the acting motor of creation and providence, ever operating in the region behind phenomena, the originating cause of all energy, all life, all thought: it means that Christ 'in becoming Incarnate did not desert the rest of His creation,' but is the quickening impulse of all that is best in what we call modern civilisation, the nourisher of new graces in the ever-widening circles of the family, the society, the state, the inspirer of art and literature and morals and government, by lifting them all into a higher atmosphere of hopefulness than was ever possible until He came, 'the head over all things, to the Church, the Fulness of Him which filleth all in all.'

Again, when we come to deal with the Supremacy of Christ in relation to the realm of Philosophy and Law, what is the record that we shall have to consider? It will be the history of a twofold contest closed by a twofold victory—the victory of Thought, of Greek Wisdom, on the one hand, the victory of Organisation, of Roman Imperialism, on the other.

And in that history, as I have already hinted, there will be no more interesting chapters than those with which our third and fourth Lectures will have to deal. For in those two Lectures the great contrast will be brought out between Greek and Latin influence in the development of Christianity. In them we shall no doubt be taught to see how, on the one hand, with the great Greek Fathers the doctrine of the Incarnation is the central doctrine of the Faith, and is regarded as the climax and the crown of a spiritual process in the history of man dating from the creation: on the other hand, we shall learn how by Latin writers the doctrine of the Fall is in reality the central doctrine, and the Incarnation is regarded chiefly as supplying means for the remedy of a catastrophe by which Humanity had been severed from God. We shall learn, too, how with the Greek 'Faith' means spiritual vision, the insight of the soul into eternal realities, illuminated by the Holy Spirit of God, while with the Latin it means primarily assent to external authority, to dogma guaranteed by the Church. Finally, we shall see how while the Greek thought of 'Salvation,' of Eternal Life, as consisting in that knowledge of God and of Christ which carried with it the harmonious development of the whole man in the way of righteousness and truth, the bringing of the will of man into perfect obedience to the will of God; the Latin mind translated all these conceptions into quantitative estimates, Eternal Life becoming unending happiness, and Eternal Death unending woe.

In a later Lecture, that on Science, you will learn how, when the time came that the Latin Mission in the Church was practically ended, and all that was good in Augustinian theology had been absorbed by Puritan thought, and all that was useful for the magisterial discipline of Teutonic Christianity had been taken from Roman Imperialism, it was not so much from the side of the New Learning or the Higher Criticism that our modern theologians have been forced back into a resumption of Greek methods of thought. It is rather the great scientific generalisation of our day, the Theory of Evolution, which is in reality restoring to their due place in the Christian Creed those truths so clearly enunciated by Origen and the School of Alexandria, but submerged for so many centuries under the grosser theology of Augustine and the Latin Schoolmen. But I think you will also learn from that Lecture, that while the liberal theologian of to-day is ready to accept from Science as his working hypothesis the Theory of Evolution, he will desire to carry it one step further than the student of Science. The Christian Evolutionist, recognising the slow and subtle process of natural selection, as the way in which God makes things come to pass, will most surely assert that, when in the process of ages Humanity began to be evolved, an entirely new chapter in the History of the Universe was opened, in which the nascent soul of man came to be of first importance, and the animal life subordinate to it. And, above all, you will learn that the Christian Evolutionist, so far from cheapening, as the good people with narrow souls tell us, the value of human life, adds immeasurably by his scientific faith to the glory of man's destiny; because he will tell you how that faith shows that after all the grand sweep of things is from the lower to the higher, that St. Paul after all was right when he said that 'the sufferings of this present time are not to be compared with the glory which shall be revealed,' that indeed 'so widespread is the confederacy of the powers of good that no failure and no series of failures can ever leave uncertain the final Supremacy of Christ over all created life.'

Once more, in Politics, in Sociology, in Ethics, the Supremacy of Christ must also be felt—but how and when?

I have no time left now to give the complete answer. You will get that in due course.

But at least we need not forget this, that in regard to Politics the Church of the Incarnation can appeal to the Democracy as the Religion of the Fishermen who gathered round the Carpenter's Son: that in Sociology the Church of the Incarnation can point the Social Reformer to the Pattern of a Perfect Man laying down His life for enemy and for friend: that in regard to Ethics, the Church of the Incarnation can point in the crowning act of her worship to a Sacrament of Brotherhood as the ideal of human fellowship, brought thus into a Divine light, and quickened by a Divine spirit.

And lastly, of Poetry and Art let me at least repeat in this connection what I have more than once said in one form or another from this pulpit.

The function of the great Painter is in its own special province of form and colour identical with that of the great Poet. The Painter's power and gift is indeed more limited than that of the Poet, for his choice of subject is conditioned by the requirement that its treatment shall come within the realm of the beautiful. All life, all nature, is the legitimate realm of the Poet. He not only beholds the Present as it is, and discovers those laws according to which present things ought to be ordered, but he beholds the Future in the Present, and his thoughts are the germ of the flower and fruit of latest time. And all life, all nature, is also the realm of Art, limited only by the condition of beauty. The Painter, like the Poet, perceives the Infinite in things, and under the conditions of his work suggests it. But to both Painter and Poet, who is also Christian, the fulfilment of his office demands not only insight but self-control. Both need discipline, both need devotion to an ideal, both need self-sacrificing, strenuous courage. For both, in the Christian view, must be Interpreters of Life, Prophets of the Infinite. They must enter within the veil, and coming forth again must declare their heavenly visions to men. They must strive to make clear to others what their keener sensibility and penetrative insight have made visible to them. They must first perceive, and then reveal the Infinite.

And can any one doubt who, in Art, has followed the history of its development in Christendom, from the rude though tender sweetness of the early Christian mosaics, through the struggles of the Middle Ages, to the inexpressible delicacy and beauty of Fra Angelico, to the calm dignity of Leonardo, to the unearthly majesty of the Mother and Son in the Dresden Madonna, or the sublime figure of Van Eyck's Imperial Christ: or who in Poetry has traced the growth, even in our own country alone, in whatever varying measures, of the divine gift of song, from the quaint grotesqueness of Cynewulf's *Christ*, in the second half of the eighth century, down to the almost Christiad, though veiled, of Tennyson's *Idylls of the King*; can any one who has done this, I say, doubt the supreme potency of the spell which the Personality of the Christ has exercised in the realm of Poetry and of Art?

And now I must close.

For some of us, for all of us, it may be that, even with the key which the doctrine of the Incarnation gives us, it is difficult to grasp the thought of the Church of Christ as a Sovereign Society embracing in one comprehensive unity all these realms of thought and action. Your outlook rather, you may say, seems to show you a picture not of ordered beauty, but of confused colour and formless design.

Ah, well, I will only say now—Have Patience! Have Faith! It doth not yet appear what we shall be. We only know now that we are weaving at the loom of our own destiny.

'Let us take to our hearts a lesson—no lesson can braver be—
From the ways of the tapestry weavers on the other side of the sea.
Above their heads the pattern hangs; they study it with care;
The while their fingers deftly weave, their eyes are fastened there.
They tell this curious thing, besides, of the patient, plodding weaver—

He works on the wrong side evermore, but works for the right side
　　ever.
It is only when the weaver stops, and the web is loosed and turned,
That he sees his real handiwork—that his marvellous skill is learned.
Ah ! the sight of its delicate beauty ! how it pays him for all it cost !
No rarer, daintier work than his was ever done by the frost.
The years of man are Nature's looms ; let down from the place of
　　the sun,
Wherein we are weaving alway, till the mystic web is done.
Sometimes blindly ; but weaving surely, each for himself his fate ;
We may not see how the right side looks : we can only weave and
　　wait.'

CHRIST IN THE REALM OF HISTORY

'*All Power is given unto me in heaven and in earth. Go ye, therefore, and teach all nations.*'—MATTHEW xxviii. 18.

A DECLARATION and an injunction consequent on it; the Leader makes his proclamation, and the followers are to rally round and impose his Lordship on the world.

But mark the difference:—the King, the Conqueror, of this world issues his mandate when he unsheathes the sword and puts himself at the head of his enthusiastic troops; and, if he is to win the victory, he must never for an hour be lost to sight. Whereas Christ utters these words at the very moment when He is taking leave of His people, after He has been displayed dying, dead, on the Cross of shame, a servile end, when His followers are downhearted, scattered, fondly clinging to what seemed to human eyes a lost cause. The whole thing is apparently a great change of front in the moment of defeat, and the Leader, cherished and beloved, instead of remaining with the frightened flock, gives them these words, lays on them this gigantic, this appalling charge—and leaves them.

All rules of worldly wisdom are reversed; and from the beginning to this day the unfriendly prophets of the world have with one voice declared the Christian movement consequent on this farewell, and inspired by the new Spiritual power of Pentecost, to be a failure.

On two sides the Church of Christ fails in success.

First, when it follows the ways and wears the raiment of the world, and is in favour, and stands beside kings. This is one hour of failure: for the Gospel has lost its simple force. And secondly, it fails when with all earnestness we proclaim the truth, and it is accepted by the world in name and voice, and the creeds are safe, and the formulæ of salvation are used, while we fail to live the life of the Gospel, and the spirit in us is not the Spirit of the Lord.

As we look across the ages for the signs of Christ's Presence in His Church, how rarely can we catch even a glimpse of His August Person! I think it is in simple cottage homes, when toil-stained rustics lie a-dying, that we become really aware of His royal presence; it is when simple, half-unconscious acts of heroism are done that we feel His influence; it is when little children in their divine simplicity sing their sweet hymns to Christ that we know for certain He is not far away. But on the larger spheres of the world, where do we recognise His countenance? Where shall we feel sure that His self-devotion has borne fruit, and that men have grown like Him?

'You come,' cries the eloquent Hindu monk (Vivekananda) at Chicago, 'with the Bible in one hand and the sword in the other—you, with your religion of yesterday to us whose faith reaches back for thousands of years—you trample on us, you treat us as the dust beneath your feet. You degrade our people with drink; you insult our women; you pour contempt on our religion, which is better than yours, for it is more humane. And then you wonder why Christianity makes such slow progress in India. I tell you, it is *because you are not like your Christ; Him* we could honour and revere. Think you that if you came to our doors like Him, meek and lowly of heart, with a message of love, with a life of work and of suffering for others, as He did—think you we should turn a deaf ear? No! we should receive Him, listen to Him, obey Him, as we have received and followed our own inspired teachers.'

Bitter words these, but wholesome—too near the truth to be neglected by any one. And if we need another sharp reminder of our shortcomings, let us listen to another writer of the day, who observes for himself and speaks out fearlessly. His words are very startling:—but they have in them deep veins of truth; and we who are searching for the historic Christ cannot afford to pass them by.

'The history of Christianity,' says Mr. R. Le Gallienne, 'has nothing whatever to do with the teaching of Christ. The world has never tried the Gospel of Christ. If the Christian Church has exemplified but little the Christian ideal, at least it has by its mistakes proved the truth of that ideal.'

As if to give more point to these terrible words, we have Bishops to tell us that a Christianity of the Sermon on the Mount is impossible in our day; that it is a counsel of perfection to be admired, not a code of precepts to be obeyed. And if the Sermon be above us, unattainable, where then stands the Divine Preacher of that Sermon?—because He is God, are we to think Him, too, unattainable?

The truth is, the World—and we are of the World mostly—has never appreciated either the Divinity or the Humanity of Christ. We have caught, chance times, a little sight of Him, but not so as to understand or to be really influenced. The salt of the earth are those who have grace to follow Him in truth, and who do not deem Him visionary because they cannot fathom the depths of His utterances or range themselves with Him in His Divine self-abasement and lowliness. He took upon Himself the form of a slave. Has the Church ever given herself to servile work for Christ? He submitted to the shameful Cross. Have we ever taken up our cross for Him?

How do we read the high prophetic words with which the Apocalyptic seer, rapt in a vision which takes no count of time, pours out his burning soul: 'The kingdoms of this world are become the kingdoms of our Lord and of His Christ; and He shall reign for ever and ever'? (Rev. xi. 15.)

Has this vision ever yet drawn nigh to its fulfilment? We know that it has not. But then, if we have in us the faith of Christ, how can we reconcile this failure in aim with what we believe of Him? Can we by watching the progress of the Christ in History either account for the failure, or win any sure hope of future fulfilment and success? I know not. Christ said, 'When I come, shall I find faith on the earth?' (Luke xviii. 8.) He at any rate was under no delusion about it. Nor had His reception by His own countrymen been so warm as to create enthusiasm : their parties, their selfish prejudices, their persistence in misunderstanding Him, their indifference to all His works of healing, their inattention to His words—all these things showed with perfect clearness that the world was not going to accept Him readily. There is no more significant verse in the whole Bible than the words with which the Evangelist records one of our Lord's barren visits to his own countrymen at Nazareth (Matt. xiii. 58 ; Mark vi. 5, 6) : ' And He did not many mighty works there, because of their unbelief ' ; or as St. Mark phrases it, ' And he could there do no mighty works . . . and He marvelled because of their unbelief.'

It would have been an easy solution—a solution of difficulties after which we all have yearned, and which, had we had the arranging of the world, we should in our wisdom have introduced at once—to have seen Christ acting on His parting words, and assuming ' all power in Heaven and on earth.' ' Probability ' should no longer have been ' the very guide of life.' The Divine Message of blessing should have been so clear to all as to leave no place for unbelief or doubt or disobedience. The Jews, instead of refusing Christ and crucifying the Lord of Glory, would have risen with one accord to do Him honour, to do His will.

There should have been no shame of the Cross; no hopes cast down; no resistance; no struggle of darkness against the light. Jesus with His triumphant legions at His back would have swept victorious across the world; the philosophy of the East, the taste of the Greeks, the civic genius of the Roman world, the fervour of Africa, the wild woodland imagination of Germanic hordes, the warm enthusiasm of the Celts—all the kingdoms of the world would have become at once the kingdoms of God and of His Christ, and the words of the Revelation would have been fulfilled to the letter. But this has not been: and from this absence of direct and forcible proof men have gathered a belief either that our Lord was a mere man, of a high type, no doubt, yet still a mere man: or that the vision of Almighty power and goodness, the Gospel of Salvation, was never intended for mankind in general, but only for a few selected souls.

And we comfort ourselves in this twilight of ours with thinking, hoping, that in another world these matters will all be made plain, and all puzzles, all mysteries, be at an end. We are probably very wrong here too! Heaven will not be a place in which God's 'All Power' will be used so as to abolish all independence in Angel or Man—nor will His knowledge be so spread abroad as to relieve us from all effort.

We must never forget the Angels which kept not their first estate; and must always remember that Man, under happiest auspices, will never outstrip Angels, or pass at a leap from our dull mundane life to fulness of knowledge or of love. We shall still be limited and low. There is a good bit of conceit in our view of the destinies of pious folk.

All advance, in God's kingdoms of nature and of grace, is gradual, and is worked out by concurrent efforts. Even the coming of Christ, the greatest of all changes to the world, was made subject to this Law of the Almighty government of the world. The Divine Nature (which we seem to have almost lost sight of by our definings and wranglings over it) did not, in taking human nature into Himself, escape from His own Laws for dealing with mankind. In some way which we cannot explain—man cannot, God can—Jesus Christ, in coming among men, showed limitations, which the Divine Nature cannot have. A few years ago it would have been counted 'dangerous' to recognise these limitations; the orthodox closed his eyes tight, lest he should read too much in the Scriptures. Those Sacred Books again and again refer to these limitations—they lie at the base of the whole humiliation and passion of Christ.

The self-same law rules in regard to the Christ in

History. At each successive epoch His beautiful and beneficent work is hindered, dragged down by the weight of circumstances, by the character of the human beings who make up the atoms of the Church of Christ. In each successive period the ideals are the same; throughout the ages the Divine Love, the Divine Morality, the Divine Community, are set before men; and we seize now on one, now on another idea from it, accept a scrap of it, stain it with our human infirmity, and then proclaim ourselves as the true followers of the Christ. It is only by slow degrees, answering to the long evolution of the material world, that the Gospel of Jesus Christ emerges out of the darkness and confusion into which our limits, religious, social, moral, have cast it. We make our religion (as men said of the idols of the heathen) in our own likeness: not 'Man in the likeness of God,' but, the other way, 'God in the likeness of Man.' This is the education of the World's life, slow, disappointing, sad. And the Revelation of Jesus Christ is never exempt from this law.

It is this which, in his fine prophetic way, Plato foresaw when he drew his picture of the manner of God's creation of things, and the splendid theory of the impact of Form on Matter, and the reaction of Matter on Form.

In speaking of this subject we approach some of the deepest and most difficult problems of life. And if we will honestly read in History and take note, at successive epochs, of the manner of our Lord's dealings with His Church and with the World around and within it, we shall at last begin to understand how it is that the Revelation of the Glad Tidings has taken such diverse, sometimes such mischievous forms, and has so little corresponded to the beautiful simplicity of the Gospel story, and has so feebly carried out the ideals proclaimed in those sacred writings, on which we still pore without penetrating beneath the surface. Could we see deeper, we might begin to understand more about that higher life towards which the Scriptures ever point; we should begin to see something of the divine glory of our Redeemer's countenance.

One of the most gifted of our writers,[1] lately lost to us, saw this truth and puts it well:—

'The Lesson of History I think is this: *not* that all the good which might have been hoped for to society has followed from the appearance of the Christian Religion in the forefront of human life; *not* that in this wilful, blundering world, so full of misused gifts and wasted opportunities and disappointed

[1] Dean Church.

promises, mistake and mischief has never been in its train; *not* that in the nations where it has gained a footing it has mastered their besetting sins—the falsehood of one, the ferocity of another, the characteristic sensuality, the characteristic arrogance, of others. But History teaches us this: that in tracing back the course of human improvement we come in one case after another upon Christianity as the source from which improvement derived its principle and its motive.'

As another[1] phrases it: 'In a word, Christianity comes into the world not as a *Conqueror* but as a *Reformer*'—with the higher aim, that is, instead of the lower; it comes not to turn the unresisting creature out of one service into another, but to elicit the personal independent power in each and enlist it all for God and good, by the healthy action of each man's judgment and will. And Christianity rightly understood is Liberty, wherein we must 'stand fast; for therein Christ has made us free.' In this world's reckoning, what is so noble as a free nation doing right and loving right, able to do wrong but scorning such low use of liberty; resisting evil because it loves good, and laying down its life rather than lose its freedom and its sense of right? And in the due

[1] H. O. Wakeman, *Oxford House Papers*, p. 211.

development of the Christian Church, the Christian man, it is the same. God has been infinitely merciful to us, in leaving us free agents. Man is (so far as we can see) the only creature of His hand who can rise and can fall to a higher or a lower estate. And for the rise or the fall, man himself is altogether responsible.

Now, History is the study of the painful development of man's nature and character, as it influences and is influenced by its surroundings. And according as ideas, spiritual life, living thought, are strong or weak, so do nations and men have glorious or uneventful, triumphant or servile, histories. Nothing in History is so remarkable as the way in which gifted races have risen to eminence, and then have either remained stationary—as we see in the case of the Chinese or the Hindu civilisation, and perhaps still more in the Mohammedan—or have grown, culminated, and then decayed away, after the analogy of the life of individuals, as we have seen in the cases of the Greek and the Roman, and of some other nations of Europe. There are those who tell us that the confusions of our present life in England, and the corruptions which from time to time show themselves in our civilisation, are so many clear signs of decadence, proofs that we are past our prime, warnings that we must expect our doom.

Let us read it otherwise; and let us understand that as the Christian soul is the salt of the earth, so the Presence of Christ in His Church and therefore in the world is the undying power of life to men and states. We may say that all decay of states is due to our failure to build on the One Foundation.

And the reason of it? Is it not clearly this—that the Gospel of Jesus Christ has in it Life?

It brings us directly into relation with God, as a merciful Father of the world. It teaches us the highest 'altruism,' the duty of living for others, not for ourselves; and it knits us into a true brotherhood in the Church, wherein we gain fresh strength. Where the muscular force of Antæus was renewed by every touch of Earth, our spiritual force is revived by the constant touch and presence of God in Christ our Lord.

And out of these blessings springs our power of influencing the personal and civil life of mankind, and of instilling fresh vigour in flagging forms. For we must, if we be true Christians, believe in the possibilities of the human race, and in the highest development of the nature of man. And having before us the ideal of Christ, we shall be able to do our part in stemming the falling current.

At no period of the history of Christendom was

this so marked as in the centuries before the days of Constantine. In those primitive days—would that we knew more about them, and followed them more faithfully!—the new power of Christ's Gospel met the corrupt volume of the Roman Imperial Life, and saved it from entire decay. It is from this collision of the old and the new that the mighty fabric of the Papacy was born—a fabric so strangely compacted of spiritual life and worldly corruption.

The Hebrew (and to some extent it may be the Druid also) had preached the Immortality of the Soul, and the essential doctrine of the One God; the Greek had preached a religion of taste, and intellect, and civic oligarchy; the Roman had imposed on the world a terrible reign of Law and Order. Then came the divine Christ of God, and infused into these different elements a new Life, a larger Freedom, a new and genuine theory of Equality—an Equality of man and of woman, of rich and poor, of bond and free. History tells us that 'one of the first Christian Martyrs of Gaul was Blandina, a woman and a slave.'

Then the World caught hold of the skirts of Christ's robe. Under Constantine Christianity became a handmaid and an adjunct to the civil power: it certainly was not 'Church and State'—it was 'State and Church.' From this time the movement of the

Christ in History, admirably adapted for the coming impact of barbarism, and destined to help immensely the civil development of the modern world, loses its spiritual force. The power is still there: but it is hardened and corrupted by the power of this world. *Christian* persecution begins towards the end of the fourth century. Still, it was through the living power still existing in Christianity that something of the civilised life of Rome survived through the barbarous ages of the West—survived even the 'Christianity of the Sword,' which became the characteristic mark of the Gospel during the whole mediæval period.

We cannot overstate our obligation to the Monastic System of the sixth century. It was the germ of a revived Christianity. The principles of Christ's Gospel seemed at last to have met with recognition. Here were communities, social entities, with no private aims, nor personal wealth; a beneficent activity pervaded the whole body; for the first time for centuries the sacredness of toil was acknowledged, and the duty of men to labour with their hands and subdue the earth, to be pure in spirit, to live humbly and simply, to be in charity with all, to give their bread to the hungry, to be at peace within and without, to praise God continually, to show forth the Lord's death till

He come—all this was splendidly and faithfully recognised and acted on. From these monastic centres a New Life spread across Europe, and it seemed as if the Redeemer's work was at last bearing heavenly fruit. But, alas for poor human nature! No long time elapsed before the World around began to tinge and thicken up the pure Life in Community. The monks became feudal lords, they ceased to labour with their hands, they began to own private property, they had their own serfs, and in the end the Monasteries were the fortresses in which old bad customs longest survived. So, again, the principles of the Christian faith were defeated by the failure of Christian men. And all the while the alliance between the Episcopal Christianity outside the Cloister and the Feudal World grew stronger and stronger: the Church and the Franks made alliance on the warpath; and a little later the Church took the lead in the sanguinary ferocities of the Crusading epoch. Yet even after this Christ was not without a witness in the splendid effort of the Preaching Orders, especially in the appeal of the Franciscans to the working world. These devoted men were, in the outset at least, witnesses to the Brotherhood of the Gospel of Christ.

After them there was but little Life left in the Church. In the fifteenth century the ideals of Christianity seemed gone. The world was asked to choose between superstition and infidelity. It is the glory of the Reformation period that—in spite of many blemishes, and of much that we would gladly have seen otherwise—the reformers brought light, spiritual and intelligent, to thousands of simple folk, and broke for ever the bonds of old tradition.

And thenceforward the Divine Presence of our Lord has slowly grown more clear before the eyes of men. In our day there has been, in spite of the resistance of wealth and fashion, a marvellous outburst of spiritual life, and a newly revived belief in the higher mission of Christianity. It was a band of true Christian men that made slavery for ever impossible to England: it is the influence of Christ which stems the tide of drink and self-indulgence and immorality. He gives us the higher aim, and His Spirit enables us to strive towards it. Perhaps, before we have done, we shall find out that Christ was the friend of the poor, the foe of the rich, and may claim 'The Carpenter's Son' for the workingman's side.

We sadly need a 'Guild of the Carpenter' in our modern Christian world. Is it too much to say that He must become the true Arbitrator in our trade disputes? too much to declare that to Him the welfare of the cottager is as dear as the wealth of a palace? too much to say that His Spirit must soften, not aggravate, the asperities of life? must lessen, not increase, the miseries of competition? must some day teach men that Peace is better than War, and that the English are not the only people who have a right to the territories of the globe?

We may be, and are, infinitely below the true level of our possibilities. But under what other influences is any advance really taking place? We may be, and are, far below our own professions, but then our professions aim at the highest of which human nature is capable; and we may not hope to transform the world, save by the slow advance of ages.

But let it be *advance*—not *standing still*. And let it be an expression in Life, personal, social, national, of the influence for good of Him who was both God and Man. The belief in Christ has been overlaid by Christianity. Let us not be of those who prefer the Church to Christianity, and Christianity to Christ. Let us go to Him: let us be with Him; and we shall learn that down all 'the ringing grooves of change' His presence has ever saved the world.

III

CHRIST IN THE REALM OF PHILOSOPHY

'Christ, in whom are all the treasures of wisdom and knowledge hidden.'—Col. ii. 2.

IF we ask, What is Christianity? I suppose that most persons would reply, It is that system of belief and worship which has come down to us from Christ and his Apostles, and which is derived from the writings of the New Testament. And no doubt for practical purposes, for guidance and consolation, for spiritual strength, for building up Christ's disciples into an holy temple, the religion which we have received by tradition from our fathers is amply sufficient. But if we come to investigate it historically, we shall find that it is by no means identical either in substance or in form with the Christian faith as it appears in the writings of Apostles and Evangelists, but that it bears distinct traces of the various ages through which it has come down to us, and of the different races with which it has come in contact. Just as the crust of the earth is made up of various rocks representing the successive stages of the earth's development, so that in it we can trace, as it were, backwards the geological history of the globe, so the complex system which we call Christianity is the result not of a single creative act but of a gradual and continuous growth, and bears legible marks of its past history and environment. In this sense, as in others, the Church is Catholic; it is not of one age or of one race, but of all: it is not Jewish, it is not Greek, it is not Roman, it is not Teutonic; it is not the Church of the Fathers, it is not the Church of the Middle Ages, it is not the Church of the Reformation, it is not the Church of the Puritans, it is not the Church of the nineteenth century; it is simply the Church Universal, the Church of Christ.

The growth of the Church has been like the growth of the natural body. It has taken up and assimilated such elements as were suitable; it has rejected such as were not wholesome, or if it has received any such they have remained as foreign elements in the body, and have so far hindered its healthy growth. On one condition only could the Church have remained unchanged: if it had never outgrown its Judaic shell, if it had remained a mere Jewish sect, then it might have dispensed with growth, but it must soon have died. The development of doctrine, which Cardinal Newman maintained in the interest of the Church of Rome, is now acknowledged to have been a factor in the Church's life from the beginning. Christ our Master gave us not a theology but a life: He taught by word of mouth and by healing act; He proclaimed the good tidings of the Kingdom of God. But when the leaven of the Christian faith came in contact with heathen thought and life, at once it began to ferment in a new direction; at once the question arose, What is the relation of the new faith to other systems of thought? With regard to Judaism, the question was simple: Abraham was the father of all them that believe, though they be not circumcised: the Law was a tutor to bring men to Christ. But what of the Greek philosophy? Was this to be treated as altogether hostile? was it to be denounced as profane? or did this too stand in any relation to Christ? It was a question of momentous importance. For if the Christian faith could not lay hold of and assimilate all the treasures of wisdom and knowledge which had been slowly accumulated in the ages before Christ; if all the past history of the race had been a dreary blank, unlightened by any gleams of the coming dawn; then men might reasonably have said to the preachers who claimed their allegiance to Christ, 'This Christ of yours may be the Messiah of the Jews, may be the King of Israel; but He is not the Light of the World, He is not the King of Men.'

The place where this question first became a burning one was the city of Alexandria. When Alexander the Great founded the city in the fourth century before Christ, and called it after his own name, he settled in it a large colony of Jews. This brought the Jewish mind for the first time into contact with Greek philosophy and speculation. The effect of this was twofold. On the one hand, a certain number of Jews forsook the traditions of their fathers and broke altogether with the Mosaic Law; and, on the other hand, many, without abandoning the religion of Israel, had become disciples and students of the Platonic philosophy. Thus, when the first preachers of Christianity came to Alexandria they found a society of Jews, professing allegiance to the Law of Moses, but penetrated with Greek ideas and combining Jewish observances with Greek philosophy. An admirable specimen of the Græco-Jewish literature of this time is the Apocryphal book of Wisdom. Here, then, the faith of Christ crucified found itself face to face with heathen wisdom and civilisation. Happily, the Church had wisdom and faith to recognise her opportunity; she frankly accepted the learning and culture and philosophy of the Greeks; she founded at Alexandria a great school of Christian philosophy, among whose first teachers the names of Clement of Alexandria and of Origen are prominent; she boldly grasped and asserted the great truth declared in later years by St. Augustine,[1] that a good and true Christian will claim truth as his Master's wherever he may find it. The principle of adapting the presentation of the Gospel to the mental condition and aspirations of various races had long ago been sanctioned by St. Paul, who adopted an entirely different tone of argument in addressing the Jews of Antioch, the simple heathen of Lystra, and the cultivated philosophers of Athens;[2] and who boldly proclaimed:[3] 'To the Jews I became as a Jew, that I might gain Jews; to them that are under the law, as under the law, that I might gain them that are under the law; to them that are without law, as without law, that I might gain them that

---

[1] Aug., *De doctr. Christ.* ii. 18. *Quisquis bonus verusque Christianus est, Domini sui esse intelligat ubicumque invenerit veritatem.*

[2] Acts xiii. 16; xiv. 15; xvii. 22.

[3] 1 Cor. ix. 20.

are without law. I am become all things to all men, that I may by all means save some.' He had said to the Ephesians[1] that Christ had come to break down the middle wall of partition between Jew and Gentile, that He might make in Himself of the twain one new man. And it followed from this that each, Jew and Gentile, had his contribution to bring to the one new Man. The Jew brought the element of worship. 'O God, Thou art my God; early will I seek Thee. My soul thirsteth for Thee, my flesh also longeth after Thee. Have I not remembered Thee in my bed, and thought upon Thee when I was waking'—words like these of the Psalmist could never have been written by a Greek. On the other hand, the Greek brought as his contribution culture, art, science, philosophy. Jews, said St. Paul, desire a sign, and Greeks seek after wisdom. It was these two elements, the element of worship and the element of wisdom, that were welded together in the School of Alexandria, and that resulted in the Greek type of Christianity. Alexandria, as it has been well put by Neander,[2] was the birthplace of Christian Theology.

It is in the writings of Clement of Alexandria that

[1] Eph. ii. 14.
[2] *Church History* (Eng. trans.), vol. ii. p. 227.

we find the relative position of the Jew and the Greek most clearly brought out.[1] As the Jew had the Law, so, says Clement, the Greek had philosophy as a schoolmaster or tutor to bring him to Christ. Before Christ's coming, philosophy was necessary for the Greeks as a means of righteousness: now it was useful for godliness, as a preparatory instruction for them that receive the faith. God had from the beginning been educating mankind: He educated the Jews by the Law, the Greeks by wisdom or philosophy, as a preparatory dispensation, which was fulfilled and summed up in Christ. Even the worship of the sun, moon, and stars had been given or permitted in order to lead men up to the worship of the Almighty Creator. Christ was the light that had lightened all men; He was the Author of all good, all wisdom. The crude conceptions of ancient religions were not mere errors, but partial truths: the divine Logos, shed abroad everywhere like the light of the sun, had enlightened the souls of men from the beginning. All things—the Law and the Prophets of the Jews, the wisdom of the Greeks, even the superstitions of heathenism—led up to Christ, the

[1] *Ἦν μὲν ὦν πρὸ τῆς τοῦ Κυρίου παρουσίας εἰς δικαιοσύνην Ἕλλησιν ἀναγκαία φιλοσοφία· νυνὶ δὲ χρησίμη πρὸς θεοσέβειαν γίνεται, προπαιδεία τις οὖσα τοῖς τὴν πίστιν δι' ἀποδείξεως καρπουμένοις. ἐπαιδαγώγει καὶ αὐτὴ τὸ Ἑλληνικὸν, ὡς ὁ νόμος τοὺς Ἑβραίους εἰς Χριστόν.

desire of all nations, the fulness of Him that filleth all in all.

It is obvious what a far-reaching principle this was. So long indeed as the Church consisted mainly of Jews or proselytes, it was natural that the Jewish dispensation should be regarded as the preparation for Christ; but when, as at Alexandria, the Christian faith claimed the allegiance of a race by whom the Jews were looked upon as an obscure and not very enlightened nation, it was natural to ask, Has God, then, for all these ages manifested Himself only to this small and exclusive people, and has He left Himself without witness for the more progressive and enlightened Greeks? And when it was replied that the wisdom of Plato no less than the Law and the Prophets was a revelation from God, that philosophy was given to the Greeks as their special covenant, as a stepping-stone to the philosophy which is according to Christ, it followed that Christianity has its roots not only in the soil of Judæa, but also in that of Greece, and that for Christians, too, it was a duty to seek after wisdom by meditation, by inquiry, by reasoning.

I have said that Christian theology had its birth in Alexandria. When the Christian faith, as it had been delivered in its rudimentary form by the

Apostles and their earliest disciples and followers, was brought into an atmosphere charged with Greek thought and speculation, it was inevitable that it should be profoundly modified by its new environment, and should take new shapes and colours. The baptismal formula, involving a belief in the Father and the Son and the Holy Spirit, could no longer remain in its undeveloped simplicity. What is the nature of the Godhead?—what is implied in the Sonship of Christ?—what is His precise relation to the Father?—if He is God, how is He also Man?—if He is Man, how is He also God?—is the Holy Spirit an influence merely, or a Divine Being?—in what relation does the Spirit stand to the Father and the Son?—these are questions which to the earliest Christians in the first freshness of their faith would have appeared superfluous or even shocking, but to which the keen and subtle intellect of the Greeks demanded an answer. And so the age succeeding that of Clement and of Origen was an age of eager controversy on the central mysteries of the faith. The doctrine of the Logos, the Divine Word or Reason, familiar to the Alexandrian School in the writings of the Jew Philo, had been consecrated for Christians by the Evangelist St. John, and had been expounded and enlarged on by Origen; and from it sprang the great controversy known by the name of Arius. The turning-point of the controversy was the question, Was Christ divine in the sense of being one with, and equal with, the Father? or, as it was at last formulated, Was He of *one* substance or of *like* substance with the Father? It would be neither possible nor edifying to go into the history of this controversy: it is enough to say that at the great Council of Nicæa, summoned by the Emperor Constantine in 325, the Arian view was condemned, and a creed was promulgated, the original of our Nicene Creed, defining Christ as Very God of Very God, begotten not made, being of one substance with the Father.

This was the great characteristic work of the Eastern Church—the bringing out in its full importance and significance of the doctrine of the Incarnation; the developing all that was involved in St. Paul's declaration that in Christ dwelleth all the fulness of the Godhead bodily, and that in Him we are made full, who is the head of all principality and power: the teaching that the Eternal Son was made man, not as a kind of after-thought in order that He might redeem men by His death, but as part of the everlasting purpose which God had purposed before the foundation of the world. That is what is meant by the clause in the Nicene Creed—Begotten of His Father before all worlds; that Christ was, as St. Peter says, foreknown before the foundation of the world, but was manifested at the end of the times for our sake. Eastern thought concerned itself mainly with the ineffable Godhead—with God as He is from eternity; Western thought rather with God in His relation to man, with the Atonement, with man's free will, with the organisation and sacraments of the Church. The East was the founder of theology, the West of anthropology.[1]

It is not just to say with Gibbon that the whole Christian world was divided on the question of a single diphthong—Homo-ousios or Homoi-ousios—of one or of like substance. Thomas Carlyle, little as he cared for the technicalities of theology, yet saw with that penetrating insight of his that the essence of Christianity was really at stake,[2] and that the victory of Arianism would have been the dethroning

---

[1] It has been excellently remarked, however, by the late J. G. Lonsdale, in his recently published sermons, that 'Theology is also anthropology'; *i.e.* that we can only know God as He comes in contact with humanity. *Cf.* St. John i. 18. Θεὸν οὐδεὶς ἑώρακεν πώποτε· ὁ μονογενὴς υἱὸς . . . ἐκεῖνος ἐξηγήσατο.

[2] 'He perceived Christianity itself to have been at stake. If the Arians had won, it would have dwindled away to a legend.'—*Life in London*, vol. ii. p. 462. Quoted by Gore, *Bampton Lectures*, p. 91.

of Christ. For when once the question had been raised, when once the mysterious relations of the Godhead had been submitted to discussion and reduced to logical formulas, it was no longer possible to remain in a purely devotional attitude towards him; Christian worship was henceforth incomplete without a formal creed. And it has been well pointed out by an American theologian[1] that the doctrine of the Trinity as formulated at Nicæa was the fulfilment of all that was true in Greek philosophy. 'In the idea of the Eternal Father, the Oriental mind recognised what it liked to call the profound abyss of being, that which lies behind all phenomena, the hidden mystery which lends awe to human minds, seeking to know the divine. In the doctrine of the Eternal Son revealing the Father, immanent in nature and humanity as the life and light shining through all created things, the divine reason, in which the human reason shares, was the recognition of the truth after which Plato and Aristotle and the Stoics were struggling—the tie which binds the creation to God in the closest organic relationship. In the doctrine of the Holy Spirit, the Church guarded against any pantheistic confusion of God with the world by upholding the life of the

[1] Allen, *Continuity of Christian Thought*, p. 92.

manifested Deity as essentially ethical or spiritual revealing itself to humanity in its highest form, only in so far as humanity realised its calling, and through the Spirit entered into communion with the Father and the Son.'

We see, then, that the idea of the threefold nature of God, though latent in the Christian consciousness from the beginning, and involved in the Baptismal formula and in many passages of St. Paul's writings, was yet not distinctly brought out until the Christian tradition came into contact with Greek thought. In this sense it is quite true that Christian doctrine has been the subject of development. The treasures of wisdom and knowledge, which, as St. Paul says, are in Christ, though hidden, were only brought to the light little by little: they were dug out by the labour of human thought, and shaped and polished by discussion. And are we to set limits to this development of Christianity, and to say that it was legitimate in the fourth century, but now all the treasures of wisdom and knowledge are brought forth, the mine is worked out, there is nothing left to reward our toil in these later days? Surely not. Surely God has not ceased to teach the hearts of His faithful people by the sending to them the light of His Holy Spirit. Surely if the Christian faith took new forms when it came in contact with the vivifying influence of Greek thought, we may confidently hope that it will put forth no less vitality in an atmosphere charged with ideas which seem likely to take shape in a transformation of our social system. 'It is not incredible,' says Bishop Butler, speaking of the Bible, 'that a book which has been so long in the possession of mankind should contain many truths as yet undiscovered.'[1]

But it may be said, Granting that the truth in the earlier ages of Christianity needed to be unfolded and developed, surely for us the possession of fixed creeds forbids the thought of any further development. I think not. Let us look for a moment at the origin and growth of creeds. The earliest form of profession of faith was, as we might expect, that required for Baptism. The question was asked of a catechumen who sought to be baptized, Dost thou believe in God the Father Almighty? Dost thou believe in Jesus Christ? Dost thou believe in the Holy Ghost? This was gradually expanded into the Roman or baptismal, or, as we call it, the Apostles' Creed. It was not, however, used in public worship, nor does it appear that any creed was so used[2] until the sixth century,

[1] *Analogy*, part ii. chap. iii.
[2] Not till the Third Council of Toledo, A.D. 589. See Lumby's *History of Creeds*, p. 101.

and then it is at the Celebration of the Eucharist, as a declaration that they who had made profession of their faith at their Baptism continued in it grounded and settled. The use of creeds in public worship originated apparently in the East, and accordingly it is the Eastern form of creed—the Nicene or Constantinopolitan—that we recite in the Communion Office. When people speak of the proposal to discontinue the use of the so-called Athanasian Creed in our services as something that must not even be discussed, it would be well to remind them that in the earliest centuries of the Church, in the ages of St. Augustine and St. Athanasius and St. Chrysostom, no creed at all appears to have been used in the worship of the Church.

Creeds, then, in their earliest and best form were simply elementary statements of Christian belief, to be made by candidates for Church-membership at their baptism, and were not designed for the purpose of restricting freedom of thought and inquiry within the Church. Even the Nicene Creed, technical as are some of its articles, and intended as it was to exclude Arius and his followers from the Church, is to us who rehearse it not so much the denial of a heresy as the triumphant confession of the Christian faith in the Incarnation. Creeds are valuable to us, not so much for their reference to past controversies and past heresies as for their relation to the present and the future: our belief in Christ is not a dogma fenced about on this side and on that side with negations, but a living faith in the living God: the true expression of our Christian belief should be, not, 'This is the Catholic Faith, which except a man believe faithfully he cannot be saved,' but, 'Lord, to whom shall we go? Thou hast the words of eternal life: and we have believed and know that Thou art the Holy One of God.'

And if we are thus drawn to Christ as His disciples; if we know Him that is true, and are in Him that is true, even Jesus Christ; if we walk in the light, as He is in the light,—then we need not fear lest the light of modern thought or modern science should obscure the Gospel of Jesus Christ. All truth is of God; it is St. James, the most conservative of all the Apostles, that declares that 'every good gift and every perfect boon is from above, coming down from the Father of lights'; and St. John speaks of our Lord as 'the true light which lighteth every man.' We sometimes congratulate ourselves that we live in an age of enlightenment, an age when every system and every institution and every tradition is submitted to the test of inquiry: and men are sometimes inclined to think that the new light is destined to supersede the old. But let us possess our souls in patience; let us not hastily, or without good cause, set aside the faith which we have received, and which has fed the spiritual hunger and thirst of hundreds of generations; let us ask God to give us the spirit of wisdom and understanding, to lead us into all truth. And let us remember that knowledge, after all, the knowledge of the intellect, is not the one indispensable thing. 'For, indeed,' to use the words of Dean Church, 'Christianity is not speculation or anything speculative. "The Kingdom of God is not in word, but in power." It is not satisfied even with abstract truth. It must be life, or it is nothing. It has, of course, it must have, a philosophy. But the moment it is treated merely as a philosophy, the idea and meaning of it perishes in our hands. The "Kingdom of God," if it is the Kingdom of God, is a religion, a loyalty, a power, an influence, a service; conquering, quickening, stimulating, controlling man, his soul, his will, his character, his fate and history.'[1]

Yes: to understand all mysteries and all knowledge is a poor thing, compared with that knowledge of God which consists in loving and serving and striving to be like Him. And this, no criticism, no inquiry can touch.

[1] *Cathedral and University Sermons*, p. 225.

'Say ye : The spirit of man has found new roads,
   And we must leave the old faiths, and walk therein ;
Leave then old forms, as ye have left carved gods,
   But guard the fire within.

'Bright, else, and fast the stream of life may roll,
   And no man may the other's hurt behold ;
Yet each will have one anguish—his own soul
   Which perishes of cold.'[1]

---

[1] Matthew Arnold's Poems : 'Progress.' I have ventured to modify the third line in quoting it, as the original form, 'Leave then the Cross,' seemed liable to misconstruction. The tenor of the whole poem shows that his meaning is, 'if you must give up the letter, at least see that you keep the spirit.'

IV

CHRIST IN THE REALM OF LAW

'But we know that the law is good, if a man use it lawfully.'
1 Tim. i. 8.

SOME of the most remarkable discoveries in science have entered the mind, as it were, suggestively or by analogy from some other calling in life. These sidelights of science, or broken lights, as we may call them, steal in unexpectedly: broken lights in a double sense, we may call them, since they help to break up into fresh groups what seemed so fixed and uniform that we had forgotten perspective and taken shadows for substances, until we needed a new point of view altogether. It comes to the same thing if we say that in theology our mental concepts are never to be taken for the realities themselves of things unseen and eternal. What is meant by a hard theology is that bloodless account of God, as dealing with certain abstractions, such as sin, righteousness, and so forth, and as regarding His creatures as guilty or innocent, according as certain conceptions of guilt and innocence

—purely forensic, let us add—are assigned to them. This is that cast of theology which has come down to us, in the West, in almost an unbroken tradition of Roman law, which has overshadowed and thrown into the shade those brighter, more benignant conceptions of God's Fatherly character which have become the cherished convictions of our day. It is strange to think how that phrase, 'the reign of law,' has changed places in science and theology in our day. The reign of law is, in science, regarded as its most cherished conviction. By slow degrees, as it were, and at the end of a hard-fought battle, the age has settled down to accept without dispute this notion of the reign of law. All science is without exception uniformitarian. The man who disputes this, and flinches from the phrase, 'the reign of law,' is at once put out of court. He was either born in the pre-scientific age or he is still in the theological or the metaphysical stage of thought, and is not yet enfranchised into the purely positive stage. The reign of law is now the dominant notion in science, and we may say of a student of science that he has not broken the shell of his subject until he enters into and accepts the phrase in its entirety. Now, strange as it may sound, the reign of law in theology was an accepted notion ages before it had occurred to men of science to fly this flag. In this respect science and theology have changed places as time went on—or, to speak more distinctly, the catchwords of the one school have passed over and become the catchwords of another school entirely opposed. As long as Roman theology reigned without a rival in the West these legal conceptions of God overshadowed every other. In the East we admit that it was otherwise. There a milder and more intuitional and directly spiritual conception of God shaped the minds of men. But in the West, with scarcely an exception, the magisterial conception of God as our Maker and Lawgiver, just and stern, shaped the minds of men, and laid the foundation of those plans of salvation and schemes of imputed righteousness on which bodies of divinity have been constructed.

Now, singular as it may sound, the reign of law is as much out of date in theology as it has become the fashionable phrase in science. Who cares to think of God as our great 'Lawgiver'? Who regards the law any longer as more than our schoolmaster to lead us unto Christ? The last word of theology is like that of the apostle, 'Show us the Father, and it sufficeth us.' Men have silently dropped, in the West as much as in the East, the Roman notion of a lawmaker. That God is a great

Magistrate ruling according to a code and enforcing it by a scheme of rewards and punishments, seems to us too bare and bald a conception to draw our souls to Him any longer. The whole evidential school of last century has been described as a jury-box kind of religion. It rests, as Paley puts it, on the testimony of twelve honest men, and, as this jury is agreed and unanimous, its verdict is able to support the most suspicious and even supernatural class of truths. Much of this has long since been swept off to the theological lumber-room, and we need not slay our slain or call up for judgment the dead and forgotten worthies of the old evidential school. But at least it remains true that the reign of law is no longer a theological catchword, but the same is true of science, or rather the two have changed places. Instead of the reign of law in theology, we speak of grace and forgiveness. 'Mercy rejoiceth against judgment.'

Nor have we far to seek for an explanation of these changed conceptions—law in science has displaced law in theology as the reigning idea. But the term 'law' has also undergone a silent transformation. By law is now meant no longer some arbitrary appointment—a statute or judgment enforced by a penalty and resting on enactment as its ultimate ground.

We have dug down deeper; we have gone beyond *lex* and got at *jus* as the ultimate ground of law. No one ever used the term *lex gentium*, but from earliest times a sense of a *vera lex, recta ratio, naturæ congruens, constans, sempiterna,* has engraved itself on men's minds as the basis of that *jus gentium* which we improperly describe as international law. We have outgrown, in a word, the limited sense of law as mere code, or statute law, laid down by the State Legislature and enforced by the executive, and as carrying little or no sanction beyond the express penalty laid down in the code. Law in the mere Act of Parliament sense is no longer the keynote to the phrase 'reign of law' in science. It is law in the sense of *jus*: that which is inherently right, based on eternal and immutable morality—that memorable phrase of Cudworth, which we lay stress on here. Law is in that sense that which is necessary, and not dependent on any arbitrary will. Hence it needs no sanctions, calls for no penalties—it has one sanction, and one executive. Some of our deeper thinkers, as for example Bishop Butler, have had a glimpse of this deeper sense of law. When he speaks of natural law he uses the term in the exact sense of modern science. By the law of gravity, for instance, we mean that property which is inalienable from matter by which it attracts and is attracted—one body to another—in proportion to its bulk and density. Here we have a law which is necessary and eternal, and which is quite the same whether we hold it to be the appointment of an Eternal Mind, or whether we leave out of view the Deist's account of the universe. Deist and Atheist are agreed in understanding the term 'reign of law' in the same sense.

Now, theology is transformed as soon as we begin to understand reign of law in the same exact sense as the term law is understood by men of science. It is the working-out of an unchangeable order of things by which it is 'well with the righteous and ill with the wicked.' As to penalties or rewards and punishments hereafter, this we regard as antiquated and out of date. Such a term as lawgiver, lawmaker, is only excusable as an anthropomorphism. It is a coarse metaphor from the path of jurisprudence among men when we break up mankind into classes. There are legislators and magistrates; these make up the legislative and creative branches of the administration, and beyond these there is the mass of the people, whose duty it is to obey the law and keep clear of its penalties. It is no small gain in our day that theology is working itself clear of this crude conception of law on which Paley laid such stress in his day. We are no longer taught that it is our duty to fear God and to keep His commandments, because God will send us to hell for ever if we fail to fear Him or come short in our standard of duty. The reign of law in science has silently corrected these bare and bald conceptions of law in theology. The two now stand abreast of each other, and we hail now the dawn of a better, brighter day, in which we see a conception of law strained of these penalties of the Roman magistrate, and in which God is set on a throne judging right, but with no thunderbolt, no needless apparatus of rewards and punishments to terrorise mankind and bring them to His footstool in a slavish spirit of obedience to His absolute commands.

Now, one of these side-lights in theology has come in from considering the change from Roman to Greek conceptions of law. Of all races in the world the Roman was under the strictest conceptions of law. We think of them at first as a military race. Soldiering seemed to be in their blood. When the Roman was at his games, those gladiatorial fights, unknown in Greece or elsewhere, formed the fitting stimulus. But this hard ruling race had another passion, and this was for litigation. They delighted in the very forms of law, and some of their civil ceremonies took shape, as it were, in an imaginary suit between debtor and creditor. Where the life was not taken up with details of the camp, then it turned to the forms of law, and to this day the majesty of Roman law is with us. Her armies are broken up, her empire is a tradition of the past, her temples are desolate and her cities wasted and gone, but Roman law still abides. The Code of Justinian lies at the base of all civil law, of which canon is only a version modified to suit ecclesiastical needs. With this commanding sense of Roman law, to which the Latin mind lent itself quite naturally, can we wonder that the theology of the West was deeply tinctured with conceptions drawn from this source? The Latin fathers may be described as jurists who had turned their attention to theology. Naturally enough, their theology took a judicial form. The shadow of Roman law was over them. Sin was not so much a transgression of the law within, a violation of the eternal order of things. It was looked on as a transgression of statute law, a breach of a code which carried with it corresponding penalties. Out of these there grew inevitably the mediaeval theory of atonement based on a principle of distributive justice, and assuming the law of equivalence, *i.e.* so many stripes for so much transgression. I am not concerned here to discuss the truth or falsehood of this or any theory of atonement. I have only to point out that this became the prevalent theology of the West, where without an exception a notion of satisfaction or expiation based on a magisterial theory of God was the point of departure. I need scarcely point out that this theory of the West took no hold of the East, where men's minds were directed in a totally different channel. There they set out with the concept of the Eternal Logos, the mind or wisdom of God, whose dwelling was in the mind of men.

So innate was this Logos or inner light of men, that the doctrine of the Incarnation was never, in the East, the same stone of stumbling and rock of offence that it has always been in the West. There, men's minds had an august anticipation and foreshadowing of the ineffable mystery. It is well to lay this thought to heart, and to turn it round and look at it in every light. Monotheism is a truth, but a truth to be held in its proportion to other truths. There is a proportion of the faith, and every man is to prophesy according to the proportion of the faith. But if we are not on our guard, one truth may so seize hold of the mind as to leave no room for another. It may dwarf all other truths and so possess the mind as to lead to a fanatical exclusion of every other. So it was with Monotheism in the later Jewish age. The race had witnessed for so many centuries that they were an elect race in possession of an exclusive jewel of truth, that Jehovah was God alone, and that He knew none other. They became severe Monarchians, and as Monotheists they had degenerated into a kind of Monarchian heresy. It was the same with their kinsmen the Arabs. When Mahomet learned this truth of the Jews his mind lost its balance, and he became, as was said of later Pantheists, God-drunk. Between man and God there was an immeasurable abyss. Between creature and Creator there was no conceivable link. By no act of condescension could the Eternal bow Himself to be found in fashion as a man. Never could the finite swell up into the infinite.

> ' He sits on no precarious throne,
> Nor begs the borrowed right to be.'

This severely Unitarian creed of Jew and Moslem alike found an impassable barrier in the Christian doctrine of the Trinity. We need go no further for an explanation of the rejection of Christ by Jew and Moslem alike; and, remembering this, we must also take account of the cause of this rejection. Truth has to be presented full-orbed. If there be any segment or aspect of truth in shadow, the mind loses the sense of harmony. It intuitively, then, knows a mere dogma from a divine truth. Dogma is of mere authority; truth seeks no better voucher than itself. It is seen in its own light, and self-evidenced as the truth, the whole truth, and nothing but the truth. The whole West, then, in effacing the doctrine of the Eternal Logos, one with God and innate with man, lost the true ground on which to base its belief in the Incarnation. It took up the line of a sterile Deism, which cut it off from all true communication of God with men. Then it had to set up a whole apparatus of proof to support the unstable building. Revelation by means of a book, and inspiration as of holy men of old. Miracles were signs from heaven, but they failed to convince that wicked and adulterous generation. For when it had cut itself off from the true fount of Inspiration, God no longer revealed Himself to men as in primitive and better times, when God walked with men and talked with them as a man does with his friend. Instead of a spiritual religion, resting on spiritual affinities and our inalienable sense of kinship with God and of God with us, there is a religion of covenants and contracts, resting for support on formal contracts, and liable to interruption by breach of contract on either side. Such a religion of the forum, not of the family hearth, fails in the one essential element of a spiritual religion. It lacks spontaneity; its one support is authority; and such as are its foundations, such is its superstructure.

It was not accidental, thus, that the Church of Rome should externalise the faith—first transform it into a cult, then interpret it as a creed. Historians have generally taken the external account of the matter. They see that the claims to supremacy in Rome lay in her being capital of the known world. All who bowed the neck to her military yoke were equally ready to submit to her spiritual supremacy. But they have failed to see that she only began to push her pretensions to spiritual supremacy when she had yielded up all claims to be the mother-city of the world. If her political supremacy led to her spiritual, why is it that as the one declined the other grew in importance? The cause lies deeper; it lies in the genius of the Roman people, for a law-made religion naturally develops into a hierarchy, and finds itself at home in a dominant and dogmatic notion of things. The Roman claim to supremacy lies elsewhere; it lies in the instinct of the Latin mind to run out into forms. The genius of the Greek mind took on a different type. It clothed itself in art forms, it sought out and found expression to its best thoughts in philosophical terms. The one used the language of the forum, the other that of the academy. Rome's religion was a law-made, law-defined religion; that of Greece was a type of philosophy, resting on accuracy of expression and precision of definition. We need not wonder that the two Churches of the East and West drifted asunder, and soon had little or nothing in common. Catholic and Orthodox, they clung to their respective watchwords, regardless of any higher, deeper unity; and as they sowed so they reaped. All our inheritance of dissension and confusion came down to us as an evil legacy of a past long forgotten. None of us can escape these traditions, or cut ourselves clear from them. They cling to us, and like the corpses of men drowned days ago they start up in mid-stream, as horrible apparitions of long since forgotten misdeeds. It alternately amuses and amazes us to see the readiness with which men step into this *damnosa hereditas* of Catholic antiquity. Church history has often been written in a dull, uncritical spirit. Men have failed to see these rifts in the lute of Catholic consent. It fails to make one music as before. Now we see that Church history is only a part, and that not the largest part, of the general culture of nations. We discover that the Latin mind had its traditions, and Greece and Alexandria another set, not easily harmonised together. The Empire also powerfully affected these traditions, it almost made and moulded them; till at last, in its degenerate type of Byzantinism, the State almost swallowed up the Church, or produced one huge conglomerate known as Byzantinism.

It would lead us into a department of special research if we followed out the later developments of civil and canon law. Roman priests soon saw that a wide field opened to them if they drew up Church law on the exact pattern of the civil code. This they did not fail to do, and the School of Bologna soon rose to eminence for its copying only too servilely the rescripts and precedents of the civil law, and making Papal law to be a faithful copy of that of the Emperors. The forged Decretals of Isidore lent themselves to the double fraud; and so down to the Reformation, and for a long time after, Roman law, canon and civil, ruled the world. Its two branches lent themselves to this usurped authority.

We have now reached the goal towards which we have been aiming. 'What the law could not do': this is the theme of the Apostolic teaching. Strange that the Nomothetes of the world, its conquerors and lawgivers, transformed the pure Gospel into another law, in the same way as that captured Greece, conquered Rome. In the same way it came about that Rome, having bowed its neck to the Gospel, again mastered the Gospel and made it conform to another standard. The language of Ritual is the same all the world over. It finds Christ's yoke too easy, its burden too light. So it environs it with a chain of ceremonies. The yoke of Mosaism is only broken off to be riveted again. Men love bondage. So true is that word of Shakespeare—

> 'E'en note, Lucilius,
> Where love begins to sicken and decay
> It useth an enforced ceremony:
> There are no tricks in plain and simple faith.'

The growth of ritual followed the decline of fervour in the old Evangelical Revival of last century by the same law of succession as night follows day. There are no tricks in plain and simple faith. Rome, all-conquering Rome, a second time laid her yoke on the world—not in this case by the march of Cæsar and his legions, but by the tramp of priests and ceremony-mongers, who turned the simple Gospel of the grace of God into an elaborate, awe-inspiring ritual. They transform the simple memorial festival of a dying Saviour's love into an awful mystery known as the Mass, in which *hic est corpus* became *hocus pocus* under the magic and mummery of priestly incantation. For the moment the world, the silly, sentimental groups of young lady religionists, have gone after this movement, and for the time we scarcely know where we are. But give us time to recover ourselves, and we shall soon look back with wonder that we were ever deceived so far. Like the Lady in *Comus*, some fell enchanter's drug must have deceived us, and we are lulled into a sleep of false security. But soon we shall arise and shake ourselves, like Samson, and, like the strong man bound, rend like tow these chains of the Philistines. Already the reaction against the reaction has set in; and Oxford, which gives us 'movements,' as they are called in the religious world, has gone out of its way to choose a head for its most famous intellectual centre and a successor to Dr. Jowett. It has gone to the North to fetch from Scotland the head of the College which in its very title carries a proud recollection of its origin. The Scotch King who gave his name to Balliol could have scarcely foreseen that the reaction against Roman formalism, which was only another name for spiritual despotism, would go so far as that a Scotchman, himself a distinguished student of Oxford, should be sent for to preside over this famous college. It is a sign of the times that as Pusey, Keble, and Newman were representative names at Oxford a half century ago, so in our day Jowett and Caird should take the lead in bringing Christian thought back to its true fountain-head. This is the triumph of Greek philosophy, not of Roman law. The hard, magisterial notion of religion which so long prevailed, and out of which the Reformation itself only wrought a half-deliverance, is at last being broken down. The name of Augustine is no longer a sound of awe to which we are to bow as to something which carries authority on its very front. With Augustine has passed away the whole of the Roman school: Cyprian, the sainted Bishop and Martyr; with him is Tertullian, the rugged, harsh advocate, who turned the Church into a forum, where he took up the sacred cause of Christ to wrangle over with the same licence of tongue and bitterness of speech as of an Old Bailey advocate. These three Carthaginians, Tertullian, Cyprian, Augustine, filled so large a place in Church history that they may be said to have set a distinct type of theology out of which, as by a natural process of growth, Roman theology was evolved. The Anglican school for one reason, as the Calvinist for another, would deal tenderly with this monstrous after-growth of dogmatic Christianity. I have traced it to its source in the denial or suppression of that precious truth of the Logos or interior light of men which until the rise of George Fox and the Quakers was practically a forgotten truth in the entire West. Do not let me mislead you, as if the East held on to the last to the better traditions of Justin

Martyr and Origen. The sacerdotal, ascetic temper there prevailed as much as in the West. The night of superstition and priestcraft set in and darkened the Churches of Antioch and Alexandria as much as it did those of Carthage and Rome. There is little to choose between Cyril of Alexandria and one of these Carthaginian dogmatists. The apostasy had set in. The simplicity of the Gospel had been departed from, the fine gold had become dim; and all were preparing for that mighty earthquake when a third part of the city fell, and a third part of mankind revolted from the yoke of Roman supremacy, and set up that century of sects which we are slowly living under down to this day.

But we do not despair. God's jewels may be buried; they never can be finally lost to the world. Slowly, some day, we are working back to sweeter, simpler conceptions of God. He is our Father, and all we are brethren. Liberty, Equality, Fraternity have been cynically defined as *un songe entre deux mensonges*, a dream between two lies. Equality is the dream of an age whose keynote is Democracy: but surely Liberty and Fraternity do not deserve the stinging name of lies. Liberty means, if it means anything, that man is a law unto himself—he is subject to the law within. Fraternity means that the second term, after the Fatherhood of God, is and must be the Brotherhood of Men. What right have we to preach and teach a Universal Fatherhood unless we go on to teach a Universal Brotherhood? Democracy is the maddest, most unmeaning of phrases unless it is founded on that noble sentiment of Fraternity. Let us not be ashamed of it because it has been put to such vile uses by degenerate descendants of that same Latin race who made Roman law the master-key by which they opened the universe, as Pistol did with his sword. Liberty and Fraternity are under an eclipse in our day, and we never can expect to see the truth unless full-orbed. Let us return to regard God as our Father. 'He that hath seen Me hath seen the Father also.' This is the true order of brotherhood. In a new relation to Christ we enter upon a new relation with the world at large—all we are brethren. Thus, 'lapped in universal law,' we shall at last begin to realise part of that dream of 'Locksley Hall,' long regarded as Utopian.

V

CHRIST IN THE REALM OF ART

'*I am the door.*'—JOHN x. 9.

IT is a strange text to take for a sermon on 'Christ in the Realm of Art,' but it is taken with a purpose.

For what, after all, is Art? The definitions are endless. 'The embodiment and communication of man's thoughts about man, Nature, and God. Man's way of giving utterance to his inspired thought. Man's way of glorifying his Maker.' So wrote the architect, John Sedding.

> 'Art—which I may style the love of loving, rage
> Of knowing, seeing, feeling the absolute truth of things
> For truth's sake whole and sole!'

That is the poet Browning's definition.

'Art is the expression of man's delight in the works of God. All great Art is praise.' So writes a third; a master he, who has led and is leading this England of ours to a truer perception of what art is than any prophet of the century—John Ruskin.

'Art is the first stage of the spirit to pure freedom and a knowledge of itself.' So wrote Hegel the philosopher. And when with these words in mind one hears Jesus Christ saying, 'No man cometh unto the Father but by Me'; 'I and the Father are one'; 'The glory which Thou gavest me I have given them, that they may be one even as we are one'; 'I am the vine, ye are the branches: herein is my Father glorified, that ye bear much fruit'; and again, 'I am the way, the truth, and the life' 'God is a spirit, and they that worship Him must worship Him in spirit and in truth';—then one begins to feel that Art and Religion must be one —that the soul of man, desiring by very instinct communion with the Father of its spirit, delighting as it were to express its heart towards God and bear fruit in the realm of spirit, struggling ever to be free from the bonds of the body of this death, to walk in the Spirit's fuller light, must turn to Him who is the embodiment of God's mind to us-ward, and strive, in the freedom wherewith He, Christ, alone can make us free, to realise that 'now are we the sons of God, though it doth not yet appear what we shall be,' and now and here, by all we do or say, by work of hand or eyes or heart, we would glorify our Father who is in Heaven.

It is in this mind that we become artists. For Art is after all but the expression of the idea within the mind. The beautiful is but the shining of the spirit through a sensuous medium. It is thought in size, in shape, in colour.

The first largely developed Art was the Art of builders. They wanted to express ideas in the spirit of praise, and did it by piling stone on stone. But they forgot that the more matter there was in evidence, the less the actual idea would be able to be given in its ideality; and that the very union between God and themselves, which they sought for by their Art, was frustrated in some measure by the very massiveness of the brute force of wood and stone they employed—that the very vastness of their works made the workers and their fellow-men think more of themselves and their own power, than of the God they sought to glorify.

The men who set their huge beams upon the necks of the bull-head columns in Susa, or placed the little cupboard for the sacred sistrum of the god in the mysterious darkness of its forest of vast columns at Karnak, had not realised that Art was but expression of spirit after all; and that it might minister as much, if it were false Art, to the spirit of pride and insolence of men as to the spirit of humble and joyous praise to God—that Art might be dumbly fettered and in chains to the very medium through which it strove to speak.

But the Greek sculptor got nearer to freedom. He took the material, moulded it to human shape divine, and made the marble breathe and have its being. What Polycletus did for his 'Handler of the Spear,' Praxiteles did for his 'Hermes' at Olympia. The spirit that was in men was almost audible. But the Greek found that marble was not the subtlest medium for the manifestation of the spirit: he took to painting, and the works of the Greek painters, though long since perished, save for so much as remains on their painted vases, must have allowed mind to realise itself at last. For, as Hegel says, ' Painting is alone capable of expressing the whole scale of feelings, moods, and ideas. Its medium is no longer a coarse material substratum, but the coloured plane, the spiritual play of light.'

' Music, it is true '—adds the philosopher—' is a finer medium still for the spirit in men to seek its realisation and find expression. But the tongue of Art is loosened only in poetry. Once let the poet speak, and the universal expression is possible in Art. For all the other arts return in poetry. And by means of poetry the transition of Art into Religion is possible.' It would perhaps be truer to assert that it is through the poetic idea that this transition is possible through the sensuous medium. For Art is after all man's thought about man and nature and God in line, in shape, in colour.

If Art presents ideas, Religion conceives them. The burden of all religion is, as its name implies, the binding of the soul of man to God; the inward exaltation of the soul to its Maker; the knowledge of the soul that it is in unity with God.

And whether we turn to 'the national religions of antiquity,' to 'the religion of sublimity of Judaism,' to 'the religion of beauty in Greece,' to 'the religion of political purpose as at Rome,' it will be found that Art has been throughout the handmaid of religion, in the direction of affecting this idea of unity between the soul of man and the Divine.

It was precisely because, in a more subtle way than was the case with the Bull Palace of Susa or the Hall of Columns at Karnak, the Art of the Greek also stopped short in its own magnificent wonder at itself, and kept men's hearts and eyes upon the work of men's hands rather than in leading them to think of the God who had inspired, and with whom the soul of the artist should have desired communion, that St. Paul when he stood at Mars' Hill in sight of the flashing helmet and spear of the brazen Athene and the mellow glories of Phidias upon the frieze of the Parthenon, spoke out and said in protest: 'God dwelleth not in temples made with hands, . . . seeing He giveth to all life, and breath, and all things; and hath made men . . . that they should seek the Lord if haply they might feel after Him, and find Him, though He be not far from every one of us; for in Him we live, and move, and have our being.'

But it is the glory of the Christian religion that in the revelation of Christ the Lord this very unity of the soul of man with the soul of God has been shown to be a truth; and the eternal principles whereby the Spirit in union with God expresses itself have been shown unto all men.

All Art that is Christian Art cannot but be filled with this idea of unity and with these principles in its expression of the idea; and whatever medium it adopts, the union of man with God as revealed to us in Christ will force itself into expression. Sometimes it will whisper, sometimes speak loud: but the idea of man being one with God, the idea of the great reconciliation, the idea that 'now are we the sons of God,' will be certainly present. Now this will mean that man must give to God the glory. All great Art will thus assuredly be praise.

'And it is a fact,' writes Ruskin, 'which ought to be very distinctly stated and very carefully considered, that all great Art has never been otherwise employed than in the service of religion except in declining periods.'

'All progressive Art,' he adds, 'hitherto has been religious Art, and the commencements of the periods of decline are accurately marked, in "illumination" by its employment on romances instead of psalters, and in painting by its employment on mythology or profane history instead of sacred history.' It must not, however, be forgotten how that before the decline there is nearly always an intermediate stage of Art that, though it is losing its vitality, is still capable of helping its time by very virtue of the fact that it is for public use, and intended to serve not private gain and luxury but public good.

It is no wonder, then, that at this time of day one very reverently would dare to sound a trumpet of recall, and would urge painter and sculptor alike to believe that in Art, as in other matters affecting the real life of the spirits of men, that text, 'I am the door,' was written for our learning; and to call upon Christian congregations to believe that, if all great Art is praise, we cannot any longer divorce from our houses of worship and praise, be they church or chapel or meeting-house, the fair handmaidens of God, painting and sculpture.

'I am the door.' The Venetians knew the depth of meaning contained in that saying, when they wrote it up in glory of mosaic over the great doorway of St. Mark's. But my chief reason for taking this text is that it was the one chosen by Giotto to carve above the portal of his famous Campanile of Florence.

It was not without some deep purpose that he who had grown up as a shepherd lad upon the dreary sunburnt slopes of the Apennine hills, and had been found by Cimabue in 1286, near the boy's native village of Vespignano, drawing upon a smooth stone one of the sheep he tended, and who grew up at Florence, after at Rome, after at Padua, at Ferrara, Verona, Assisi, and Ravenna, to be chief master decorator of his time, in mosaic, in sculpture and colour, beautifier of the Vatican, painter of the Chapel of the Arena at Padua,—it is not without some deep purpose that he should have earnestly desired to let the words of that Good Shepherd Christ, whom he followed and whose he was, sink into the minds of all who would ever enter that little side door which leads them into his glorious snowy-pink tower—the Campanile of the Duomo, beneath whose shadow now his dust is laid. He knew whence came his power and whither it went. Christ was to him and to his Art verily and indeed the Door.

This Giotto, one of the best all-round handicraftsmen of his time, was, if we may measure the value of Art by its moral power and original force, one of the greatest men that ever lived. His simplicity of manner and pure colour, his nobility of thought and form, his reality of intention, have been felt for good all through the centuries. And the friend of Dante and Petrarch, who fell on sleep in 1337, in the prime of his life and fulness of his honour, before the second storey of his beautiful tower had risen in the sunlight of Florence, has, in very virtue of the fact that he had recognised that Christ was the door of his Art, been able in the nineteenth century to help to regenerate our English School of Painting.

Whether they know it or not, whether they will avow it or no, our greatest religious painter and our most inspiring and thoughtful one—Holman Hunt and Watts—are pupils of Giotto.

Now, one wants to see what it was in Giotto that made him the power that he was. He was an eminently faithful man. He caught the glow from his master Cimabue of that warmth of personal love for Christ which under the teaching of St. Francis of Assisi had been felt as a flame of life through Italy.

By choice or not, his work was all religiously spiritual; but whether one gazes at the series of sculptures that represent the Old and New Testament teachings upon his tower, or at the wonderful series of frescoes in the Chapel of the Arena at Padua that set forth the Messianic story—simplicity, pathos, and reality, the truth as he knew it and felt it about the story of Him who was the Truth, the Way, and the Life, came to the front.

One could no more not expect to find Eve plying her distaff as she leaves the gates of Eden, upon the Campanile, than one could not expect the mourners at the grave of Lazarus not to be seen holding their noses, in the Paduan chapel, if Giotto is sculptor and draughtsman.

As one gazes at his Entombment picture at Padua one almost hears the heart-broken sob of the angels in Heaven weeping with agony of tears above the mourners around the body of the dead Christ; whilst, if one looks at the face of Judas betraying Jesus with a kiss, one feels a man with such a face could do no other. If one, on the other hand, turns to the face of the ascending Christ, one feels the upward-lifted hands of the Saviour have already grasped the glad and welcoming arms of Him, our Father and His Father, to whom He is ascending.

This is the Lord's doing. His Spirit demanding truth in the inward parts, made that demand on Giotto, and Giotto's soul responded; and whatsoever he did, whether it was drawing a simple circle with a brush of red paint to prove he was master of his hand—or whether it was the painting of the Nativity with the Virgin Mother turning on her couch that she may herself assist in wrapping the child in swaddling clothes and laying it in the manger, as the Gospel narrative had it—all is truth to the uttermost possibility of hand and heart and eye. Mastery of hand and mind—the Christian's self-mastery of his full powers—these are the words of the Gospel which receive such force from a study of Giotto's work.

'If any man will follow Me, let him deny himself.' Truth, Temperance, Self-mastery, ability to refuse all the thousand additions to the Gospel story then in vogue, ability to dispense with all the ornament and additions of costume effect—the jewellery of a Fra Angelico or the etceteras of an interesting background of a Bellini or Benozzo Gozzoli—to let the simple truth be set forth in ungarnished appeal to the heart; this self-restraint was learned in the school of Christ: of this Giotto was a master example and a true teacher.

It is owing to this mind of Christ 'the Door,

Christ 'the Way, the Truth, and the Life,' Christ whose Spirit still is guiding the hearts of men into all truth, that such men as Madox Brown and Rossetti lived and laboured amongst us; that we now in England have such workers as Watts and Hunt, Burne-Jones and Morris, Alfred Hunt, Goodwin, and Gilbert, and such a teacher as John Ruskin; that our time has been blessed with such revelations as Turner gave us; that your city has been made glad with that picture of Dante's dream at the hand of Rossetti, the painter-poet, or of 'The Flight into Egypt,' or as it is sometimes called, 'Christ and the Innocents,' by Holman Hunt.

Truth in the inward parts, truth in the eye and heart and hand, truth to God, to man, to nature. These truths Giotto taught and wrought for, and we are his children, entering still by the same gates he entered in to his tower of aspiration, of fame and beauty and everlasting life, by Christ the Door.

And where did this love of truth and simplicity come from?

It came forth from its hiding in the Catacombs at the call of Christ. It came down from the mosaics of the Byzantine churches.

The very idols which St. Paul preached against at Mars' Hill were in God's good time a means of giving to the Christian world a living Art for the service of religion.

There was a time when, partly because of the presence of Jewish members in the congregation whose whole training had been to have nothing to do with graven images, partly because of the Gentile converts who had turned from dead idols to serve the living God, there was a time, I say, when to be an artist meant excommunication. If a craftsman returned to his trade after having become a Christian, he was considered an apostate and denied the rites of baptism.

But all great Art is praise. The sense of a young and enthusiastic Church as it followed the great Bishop and Pastor of its soul must needs by painting and by sculpture, as well as by psalm and hymn, give God the glory; and there in the Catacombs at this day may be found the joyous figure of the young strong Shepherd, staff in hand and lamb across His shoulders, that was leading His people to safety from the ravening wolf of the world.

From that time until the fourteenth century, the artist felt his mission was divine, and that his duty lay in the path, not only of praise, but in the directing of that path, and in the interpretation through his Art of the will of God to man. Thus we read in the opening of the Statutes of the Guild of Painters of Sienna in the fourteenth century, such a sentence as this:

'But seeing we are appointed to the high duty of explaining the will of God to men, it behoves us to be ourselves holy and to attend to the divine service of the sanctuary.'

I said that early Christian Art was helped by the Classic Art of Greece and Rome. It is impossible not to see in the Orphic Christ, or Christ Shepherd, there depicted, that the artists had the Apollo ever fresh and young in their minds as they portrayed their Saviour.

That truth, 'I am come that they may have life, yea, and that the more abundantly,' it was felt, was best set forth by the vigorous abundance of life in the young, sturdy, serenely powerful Saviour and Giver of all life that those old Catacomb artists delighted to paint.

But the sorrows that fell upon the early Christians, and their sense that after all spirit was stronger than flesh, their memory of the story of Him whose countenance was marred more than any man's, had also its effect. The Lord was leading His troubled Church into all truth. Flesh might fade, but spirit should endure. Beneath rough outward form might grace be hid.

Hence, from the earliest Byzantine churches' walls, looked forth faces of our Lord, full of awe, sad and sorrowful, with nothing for which we should desire Him if we saw Him.

The medium in which these artists worked, aggravated the ugliness, the deep-lined, sorrowful severity and sourness of the face. And it was not till Christianity felt that it was a conqueror, that the Christ as portrayed in Art became a triumphant Christ.

Go to Ravenna and gaze upon the 'Christ led Captive,' the 'Christ and the Woman taken in Adultery,' the 'Christ Healing the Two Blind,' the 'Shepherd feeding the Sheep.' You will find there depicted nothing unsightly and sad or emaciated, but broad-browed beneficence, strong and tender patience in a strong and kindly face.

But if you should be able to contrast the great mosaic face of Christ in glory, blessing the people, as it was wrought in the sixth century at Ravenna—a face long and thin, with large eyes deep-sunken as if by years of pity, pain, and solicitude—with the face of the Christ in the same attitude just lately wrought in mosaic in the apsidal dome of St. Paul's, it will be evident that if the early Church of Christ at Ravenna felt that it was through much thought and care and tribulation it must enter the Kingdom, the Church of

Christ in London believes its warfare is accomplished, and that its way is one triumphant way of glory unto glory.

It is, however, to be remembered, that it is impossible to say from the religious paintings or mosaics of an epoch, what the actual condition of religious life was at the time when the Art-work was done. But it is not impossible to know whether the Art was used in the service of Religion, 'as all ancient Art was, or only as a luxury, as nearly all modern Art is.'

And as we review the ages of painting—the fourteenth century with its thought expressed by Giotto and Orcagna; the fifteenth century with its marvellous draughtsmanship as seen in the work of Leonardo, Raphael, Ghiberti, and Michael Angelo; or the sixteenth century with its masterful power of colour and painting as exhibited by Tintoret, Paul Veronese, Titian, and Correggio,—and ask yourself why it was that after—for two centuries, the seventeenth, eighteenth—that Art, except for luxury and pride, was not, one cannot but be led to believe that the reason lay just here: that Christ had ceased to be the Door, and that till a painter with the heart of faith should arise to give us 'The Light of the World' in the nineteenth century, the Light of the World so far as Art went, was quenched.

How about the picturing or setting forth the Christ who is the Door? To the student of the ages of great painting in Europe from 1300 to 1530, it must ever be a matter of surprise that through all these ages of a Faith which, whether it had lost its soul or not, was still in Christ's name and in the service of religion anxious to secure to it all the best that craftsmanship could give, the Saviour's head was so seldom portrayed with power or great glory.

With the exception of the head of Christ ascending to His Father as given us by Giotto, and the head of Christ as seen in glory in Raphael's greatest picture of 'The Disputa,' and a face of Jesus stepping from His tomb in Francesca's picture of 'The Resurrection,' one cannot see either the pathos or the power which one believes must have been in that face.

I do not forget that wonderful picture Fra Angelico painted of Christ as a pilgrim speaking to two monks, painted over a doorway (which is preserved in the gallery of St. Mark, at Florence), nor that other of the Saviour saying, 'Touch Me not,' to Mary in the Garden of the Tomb. I remember, as I speak, the face of the Christ, as Rembrandt drew Him, talking to Mary Magdalene, as seen at Berlin; or sitting with His fellow-travellers at the little wayside inn of Emmaus, as seen in the Louvre; or healing the sick in the Temple, the etching of which is known as 'The 100-florin plate.' I am not forgetful of the Christ as seen in Titian's 'Tribute Money,' nor as revealed in Dürer's 'Man of Sorrows.' But except in Leonardo's 'Last Supper,' it does not appear that any painters of the greatest painting age have given the world an adequate conception of that face which was 'the express image of the Father, full of grace and truth.'

There, however, still marvellous in its dimness, on the Refectory wall at Milan, may be seen Christ surrounded by His disciples, all of them with faces full of character and earnestness, but none approaching to that strong, sweet, unearthly face of the Man of Sorrows, who was in all his depth of tenderness a woman; 'a face'—as a friend wrote me from the place but yesterday—'full of dreamlike beauty and profound sadness that seems to say, "I am come to do Thy will, O my God; I am content to do it."'

And there at last may men feel, as they watch the breaking of bread, that He who was the true Bread of Heaven is being visibly broken before their eyes, for the life of the world.

One other face of the Lord has been revealed at the hands of a faithful servant, and of this last one dares to speak with reverence—the painter of it is still with us. It is to be seen in the Chapel of Keble College at Oxford. It is the face of the Light of the World as He stands in the frost and moonlight in a long-neglected orchard garden, at a rusty door that has been seldom opened of late. In the hand of Him who stands at the door and knocks, is a lantern symbolical of the seven spirits which are before the throne; on His head is a crown of thorns, it is true, but no more of thorns that lacerate, rather of soft leaves for the healing of the nations; and from the nimbus of light about His head and from the tender eyes luminous in the darkness goes forth a message of good hope for the light that shineth in the darkest place to the clearer day, and good assurance that even here, for that darkened and fast-closed heart, its power of appeal shall not be in vain.

But it is not only of Christ as portrayed in the realm of Art, but of the power of His Spirit in that realm, that we would speak.

What did that Spirit of Him who is Himself the Door, do, as He stood at the gate of the darkened centuries? What did Christ in the realm of Art effect?

I answer that, through the hands of the painters, He gave men their ideals of the worth of pure girlhood, womanhood, gentle childhood, and of the joy of faithful family life. He filled men's hearts with the desire for self-sacrifice. He showed men that sorrow for sin and death in Heaven and on earth is one—how the joy in Heaven and on earth over one sinner that repenteth, is one also. He peopled this earth of ours with guardian presences, angels to help men at their need. He called men, by the hands of His servants the painters, to realise the pitiful helplessness of death, and so urged men to feel they must work ere the night come when no work can be done. He bade men know that death did not end all things, and that he who died in Christ might live with Him. He set men to the task of active benevolence. The hearts of those who saw Him going about doing good and healing the sick, felt, if they would be His friends, they must go and do likewise. He urged men to believe that after death came judgment, and that wickedness and sin brought certain retribution.

He showed people that the world of nature was also a world of peace: that the flower that grew, the wild animals that ran, were here not to be trampled on or tortured, but to give men joy and to help them to be thankful to God their Creator. All this, and more than this, did the Spirit of Christ in Art.

But one other thing it did also: it taught men that the truest Art was the Art that appealed to thought, and not to lust of eye or pocket; that he was truest

workman who wrought not for gain but for love—
with sacrifice and not with care that costs nothing
—for good and not for fame.

And it showed men that the work that alone would
last eternal on earth and in the Heavens, was the
work that by its reality and sincerity, by its truth to
life and the facts of life, truth to the soul and the
facts of the soul, truth to nature and the facts of
nature, would appeal to the conscience and minds
of sincere men to the end of time, and set forward
the glory of the Father of sincere spirits.

'I am the Door,' said Christ. 'I am the Door,'
wrote Giotto on the lintel of his Campanile doorway.
Christ, the Door to all true Art, is the Christian
believer's motto still.

You ask me for examples. For purity of maiden-
hood, of womanhood and childhood, gaze on the
'Annunciation' of Giotto in the Arena Chapel, or of
Fra Angelico in the corridor of the Church of the
Annunciation at Florence, or on that other severely
simple picture with like subject in the Museum of
St. Mark in the same city; at Fra Filippo Lippi's
in the old Pinakothek at Munich, at Leonardo da
Vinci's in the Uffizi at Florence, or the sketch of
'St. Anne and Virgin and Child,' that once stirred
the City of Lilies by Arno's stream to its heart, by

its portrayal of the Holy Maid of God, and is now preserved to us in the Diploma Gallery of the Royal Academy,—and you will know assuredly that between 1300 and 1500 the modesty of maidenhood was held at fairest worth.

Go now to Francesca's 'Madonna and Child' in the Duchatel collection at Paris, the Sandro Botticelli picture of 'The Virgin and Child with St. John' in the Louvre, to Crivelli's 'Madonna' at Buda-Pesth, to the 'Granduca Madonna' by Raphael in the Pitti at Florence, to the Bridgewater 'Madonna' in London by the same artist, to the 'Visitation' by Raphael in the Prado at Madrid, and motherhood and the cares of motherhood in noblest purity will stand confessed.

Are we inclined to think little of infancy and its power to keep us reverent? Let us kneel with the kings at the child Saviour's feet, as Memling at Bruges or Dürer in the Uffizi, or as Luini at the Louvre, bids us kneel.

Do we have any doubt as to the power of the young child life to guide us and help us to be true? and do we doubt that these children have come not in utter nakedness,

> 'But trailing clouds of glory
> From God who is our home'—

that they hear in their innocence and simplicity a

happier music than falls on our ears as we march to the sound of sad heart-tap to the grave? Then let us look upon that picture that Botticelli drew of the Madonna with the child Jesus on her lap listening, with hand uplifted to ear, to the chanting of the angel chorus standing by. Then let us gaze on Cimabue's fresco of the Madonna enthroned with angels and saints on the wall of San Francesco at Assisi, or on Giotto's picture of the same in the Academy of Florence, or on the elder Holbein's 'Madonna and Child' with attendant angels in the museum at Nuremberg. And as we gaze at this last picture let us learn that the birds of the air, though two sparrows be sold for a farthing in the open mart, are all dear unto the Lord—that the very robins are welcome guests to Christian homes for Christ's dear sake.

And the next time we are tempted to wear an egret plume, which means the death of the mother and a whole nestful of young, let us think how through such artists as Holbein and Titian the Spirit of Christ bodied forth, unto a rough-hearted time, the fact that the birds of the air and the beasts of the field should be treated with reverential care.

I sometimes think that if that picture by Titian of the Holy Family, called 'The Virgin and the Rabbit,' now in the Louvre, could be reproduced and hung in our miners' cottages, their cowardly sport of rabbit-coursing might cease to exist; that the heart of the partridge-shooter would be softened if he studied that picture by Bellini, now in the National Gallery, of St. Jerome in his study. I confess that since I gazed upon Francesca's 'Nativity,' now in the same collection, I have thought kindlier of the magpie, even when seen single. Francesca may have known the old adage, 'one for sorrow,' when he painted the bird upon the rude shed's roof above the Christmas babe. He certainly did his best to remove the ban from the poor bird's family, whose manners he so well knew, when he made the inquisitive bird one of the first visitors at the birth of the Bringer of good tidings unto all.

And other things than reverent care for animals, did those old painters teach. (I say old, for we must remember how a later Italian school, through the hands of such a painter as Barocci, did, in the decadence of Art, actually lose its sense of pity for the humbler creation, as any one may know who sees 'Our Lady of the Cat' in the National Gallery.) Go and look in Venice at Bellini's 'Virgin and Child,' the latter with the pink or carnation in its hand. Watch the angels scattering their roses and rose-leaf showers into the lap of the Infant Jesus as Filippo Lippi has painted them. Gaze upon the tomb left by the risen Virgin, filled now with pure lilies, as Raphael and many another drew it. Or when you next stand before Leonardo's 'Madonna in the Grotto,' of which we have a replica in the National Gallery, note the flowers in bloom about the feet of the Virgin, and you shall feel how, where Christ is, new love for all sweet innocence may be, and the flowers of the field shall be glad for Him. The desert shall rejoice and blossom like a rose.

Do you doubt this? Go to any great Gothic cathedral—Amiens, Rouen, Rheims; that tender care for the true plant form the sculptor has left us is but another side of the tender care for all plant life that Ruskin has taught us. It is all part and parcel of His mind who said, 'Consider the lilies.'

But as you gaze at the 'Madonna' in the Grotto, you will see how, by the painter Leonardo, it has been given us to realise the power of young child-life to lead us unto prayer. St. John, the infant playmate, may hold his hand in blessing, and the beautiful woman kneeling by may point us to the praying Child Jesus at the feet of His Mother Mary; but there is such tenderness and power of appeal in that clasping of the tiny infant hands in prayer, we need none to point the lesson. A little child shall lead us.

Do we doubt of the joy of faithful, happy family life where Christ is of the household?

Gaze on the 'Holy Family' so perfect of Leonardo's school, or at Andrea del Sarto's 'Holy Family' in the same gallery, or on Raphael's 'Holy Family,' with Christ seated on a pet lamb, in the Prado, Madrid. And go to the grand ducal castle at Darmstadt, ask to see that splendid portrait the younger and the greater Holbein painted of Jacob Meyer, the Burgomaster of Basle, and his two sons, his daughters, his two sisters kneeling at the feet of his fair wife, Madonna, with her naked babe, Christ, in arms, and say if you have ever felt more truly the holiness that Christ to a united household brings, or the joy and strength that is bred from such a family confession of their Lord as here is breathed from the reverential canvas.

I have faith that it would be impossible not to have family prayers the order of any house, on whose walls a print of that picture was hanging.

But what of the suffering Saviour?

The suffering of Christ upon the Cross—this, it is true, was not painted in the early times of Art. It is singular that not till the Church grew and became

powerful did men dwell upon the piteousness of
Christ the Sufferer. In William of Cologne's 'Crucifixion,' about the year 1400, the picture is divided
into five parts, four of them filled with hugely mitred
bishops and saints. And therein it may be noted
that the angels who hover by the Lord in agony,
have all of them chalices to catch the blood that
drops from the wounds. The sacerdotal and sacra-
mental ideas underlie much of the picturing of the
Passion, and except to those who hold with sacra-
mental theories, the appeal is of small avail. But
who of us can gaze upon Mantegna's 'Crucifixion,
in the Louvre, and not feel the bitterness of the
Cross and Passion—the foul murder of the Innocent
One—nor come away vowed to follow Him, who
showed the greatest love and laid down this His
life for His friends, yea, even though it nail us to
the Cross?

Nor can we ever look upon the figure of the
Scourged Christ, with the blood soaking through
to the garment wrapped upon Him, as Tintoret,
in the School of St. Rocco, drew Him—the Lamb
before the shearers, patient and dumb—without being
filled for ever with a haunting sense of the agony
and pain that Christ then suffered for us.

Christ died so many years ago, we have forgotten

what His friends for whom He died then suffered—we are tempted to forget what any of us who are His friends must suffer, when the Lord of Glory is crucified anew, as every day He is so crucified, by the brutal hate or the careless indifference of a world that will not have Him for its King.

But Botticelli would not have his time forget it—he who painted, as we know, between 1446-1510. In the Poldi Pezzoli of Milan, and again in the old Pinakothek at Munich, you shall see sorrow as I have never seen it elsewhere painted, in his pictures of the 'Entombment.' And if ever mother think that, when she loses her dearly beloved son, hers is a sorrow unto which there was never the like, let her stand in that same gallery at Munich, before the picture Quentyn Matsys drew, and feel the pain in a heart too full for tears of her, the Mother of our Lord, who puts her cheek to the cold, dead face of Him who loved her to the end, and holds with agonised embrace the silent lips to hers—lips dumb for sorrow. Or let him gaze in the School of St. Rocco but for a moment, on the fainting figures of the five Maries at the foot of the Cross, whose very drapery is full of the expression of pain, as Tintoret felt it.

But I said that these painters also set forth that

the joys and sorrows of earth had response in heaven. The Communion of Saints and the Community of feeling of the Saints, the sympathy of Heaven for earth—this, too, was revealed by the Spirit of Christ through the hands of His servants the painters.

Was ever such joyance seen in Heaven and on earth as is depicted for us by Botticelli in the picture of 'The Nativity' in our National Gallery? Angels embracing men below, weaving an aëry wreath of song and flower and waving palm-branch; above, angels on the roof of the stall in happy benison, guiding the shepherds to the new-born Child with gracious gladness. Or at the Cathedral of Orvieto let us see the joy in Heaven of the welcoming host of angels leading the elect to sound of lute and pipe and cheering wave of hand, upward, ever upward, to their eternal home—and let us thank the painter Luca Signorelli.

Nor, since it was of Giotto we first spoke, as the fountain-head of faith in that truth that Christ was the Door, can we forget that he too felt the joys of Heaven and earth, in all that appertained to Christ and the Christ-life, were one.

Very, very bitterly did he portray the weeping of the angels above the dead Christ by the Tomb in the Garden. And very full of quiet joy did he paint the attendant hosts of the redeemed with the ascending Lord, and of the angelic messengers who point to the wondering disciples the way whither Christ is gone, and bid their hearts to follow. To this all who have ever studied the frescoes in the Arena Chapel at Padua can testify.

These artists taught that after death came the judgment. Smile as we may at the grotesquery, it must have made many a rogue shudder as he entered the door of the chief city church at Fribourg, or the northern gates of the great Cathedral of St. Louis at Rheims, to see how large a mouth hell had open for him and how gladly the devil and all his angels were seen driving in chains their servants to the monstrous jaws of the devouring dragon, or kindling the fires that shall not be quenched, for the burning of the usurers, the unjust, and adulterers. Sculptors and painters taught one lesson on this matter.

One other message comes to us from the canvases. God made the country and man made the town.

Why is it that one does not find the Virgin and her Child in palace drawing-room or in garret attic? Why are the Holy Family found not in city square or street, but always in the open country?

It was because these painters knew that the Christ's message was to simple folk; that He who had gone throughout the villages of Galilee, and returned to the mountains to rest a while, had refused to spend His last night in the busy city, but had gone off to the quiet Kedron valley down the sycamore-shadowed road, away to the peaceful olives of little retired Bethany.

A message this for us and our time, when instead of living in the country-side with sunset and sunrise through clear air, to bring us message of a purer world, whither our spirits would flee away and be at rest, we are crowding up into the brick-built Babylons and sitting in sulphurous darkness—save for the gaslit gin-palace at the corner—to 'hear each other groan.'

And this, notwithstanding the fact that agriculture, owing to the recent additions to our scientific knowledge of the earth's chemistry, and recent improvements in legitimate mechanical aids to hand-labour, has become a very complex and interesting business, capable of educating the many sides of such a many-sided handicraftsman as a good farmer or farm labourer must be.

But what has Christ in the realm of Art to say to this problem? He has to say this much, that no Art is possible, no labour is likely to be lovable and lead to Art, in which men cannot express themselves whole and sole. That the Red Indian who makes his bark canoe from first to last, the wild South Sea Islander who carves his proa-head, the Arab camel-driver who plaits the tassels and broiders his camel saddle with coarse shells, has a far better chance of having his whole sentient being called out to an expression of his sense of beauty, and a desire to give God, whom he dimly feels after, the glory of it, than are the tens of thousands of capable mechanics who are crowded in our unlovable city workshops and sleep in our unlovely city slums.

And if the true test of civilisation is, as Emerson says, 'not the census, nor the size of cities, nor the crops, but the kind of men the country turns out,' our England, for all its board-schools and its free libraries, is not turning out to-day such men as knew Giotto and went with joy to the Church of S. Marco or Santa Maria Novella to carry home the last great picture that the painter of their city had wrought.

And why? Because Joy in labour is dead!

Instead of thinking first of the work, its aim, its object, its use, its service to man, its possibility of glory to God the Inspirer, the craftsman in the factory and the ordinary successful painter at his easel, putting the last touch to the hunting-boots of the red-coat squire, or to the ringlet of the little over-dressed countess's child, has now no other interest than the wages to be paid for the work.

What Carlyle called the 'cash nexus,' what had better been called the 'cash insulator,' has come in. And the joy of service to their fellows and their God by the work of their hands has failed, helped not a little thereto in the mechanic and factory-hand's life, by the fact that he never sees the fruit of his hands' labour himself; and whilst he spends his life in making one bolt, or screw, or ratchet, or spindle, the great engine he laboured for and the cloth he helped to make, pass from him and have nothing of his own whole soul's full desire stamped upon them.

It is not that the mass of the people are ill-fed, as Ruskin has told us, that makes them discontented to-day. It is that joy in their labour has ceased under the sun, and that work, instead of being worth doing well, with a great motive of service to God and their fellows, is now done only for the money it can get. And verily we have our reward: the sin of industrial and art-producing England is finding us out.

But in the great living times of the Painters this was not so. The man who made Giotto his sculptor's tool, or paint-brush, made it from first to last. And as for the doing good work merely for good pay, the idea was abhorrent to the artist-mind, that felt in giving, not in getting, lay at once its inspiration and its very power of expressing praise to the Highest and

Holiest. Carpaccio knew that an artist should paint as a bird sings—because he must. And if you gaze upon the face of Matthew Levi, in the Church of S. Giorgio dei Schiavoni at Venice, when, leaving his money-changer's table, he steps down to meet his Lord, you will know how deeply Carpaccio felt that it is not till a man has done with the money-bags that happiness can be. Levi's face is all aglow with the new joy as he turns from filthy lucre to the Lord and Master of all poor men.

Giotto as he toiled at his great tower in Florence, though he knew that he should receive but twenty-five gold pieces at each quarter day, had no thought of other gold for his service than the sunlight flashing far and wide above the red-brown city, from his splendid tower, as long as his tower should flush with dawn or redden with the eve.

Not what he could get, but what he could give his fellows; not glory for himself and household, but for Padua and Florence and for God, did the chief architect and painter of his day seek for and work for.

'He that is chief among you, let him be as he that doth serve.' 'I am among you as he that serveth.' 'For the Son of Man came not to be ministered unto, but to minister, and to give His life a ransom for many.'

This was the voice of Christ that sounded in Giotto's ears, and sounds in the ears of all who truly follow Him.

It is the voice of Jesus that cries to the Painter, the Potter, and the Sculptor, the Architect of our day; to the guardians of our great cities; to the shepherds in our lonely villages, the carpenter in his village workshop, the mechanic in the factory or forge.

And not till it is heard aright, will captive Art break its golden chains, its silken mesh of luxury and selfishness; assert its freedom in Church, in Chapel, in Public Meeting-place, in Street, in Gallery, in Home, and in Dress; and be once more, instead of Mammon's slave, the Servant of God and of the people, the Gate and Door for Christ and Truth and Glory.

VI

CHRIST IN THE REALM OF ETHICS

'*Take my yoke upon you.*'—St. Matthew xi. 29.

One of the new features of our time is the establishment of Societies for Ethical Culture. Here in England, in Germany, in the United States, there are serious persons to whom selfish immorality is an evil to be combated, and who find it impossible to believe in the religious sanctions—as the phrase is—by which morality has hitherto been enforced. So they propose to dissociate morality from theology, and to cultivate morality by itself. And as this age is a wonderful one for societies, and can never have enough of addresses, these votaries of morality pure and simple follow the fashion or yield to the common instinct in forming themselves into a denomination and meeting together on the Day of Rest to give and receive expositions and exhortations. I believe also that these Societies of Ethical Culture have begun to follow the times in another way, and are issuing journals or magazines to serve as organs of their cause and to disseminate their views.

A modern definition of religion has described it as 'morality touched with emotion.' In this sense many of the promoters of ethical culture are willing to accept, and even to claim, religion as a part of their scheme of life. They would like to feel warmed and softened, in performing moral acts and cherishing moral sentiments. They persuade themselves that they can reject theology but retain religion. In a book of advanced views just published, entitled *The Religion of a Literary Man*, I find the sentence, 'In short, we have accomplished the inestimable separation of theology and religion.' Let me tell you what morality, or the morality touched with emotion which sometimes calls itself religion, separated from theology or belief in God and revelation, seems to me to be like.

Imagine some one coming into your garden in the early summer and looking at your flowers. He is fascinated by their beauty of colour and form; he enjoys the freshness and variety and subtlety of their fragrance. He says, 'Let us pluck off all these flowers from their stems, and gather them into baskets; we shall then have all that is precious of them, and we can adorn our rooms with their blossoms and bursting buds.' You begin to offer some protest about the roots. He, we will suppose—it is a necessary supposition for the simile's sake—declares himself to be agnostic as to the roots. He does not see them; he knows nothing of them; he refuses to be troubled by them. If you suggest that the flowers have got their life from the roots, he answers that he will find some other way of keeping them alive. He puts them carefully into vases, with their stalks in water, and makes them look beautiful; he studies the temperature of the room, he considers what sort of water the flowers will like best, and he tries the effect of putting some chemicals into it. On the second day, the third, perhaps even the seventh, he points triumphantly to the flowers: 'See how fresh they are! Some of the buds have come out more happily than they would have done if they had remained upon those old roots which we left to themselves in the garden. In short, we have accomplished the inestimable separation of the flowers and the root!' Let the illustration serve for mere suggestion.

You do not need to be reminded that the one dominant idea of all the speculations that belong to our age is that of evolution or growth. We are bidden to observe how everything that now is results as a product from causes or forces which have gone before it. Every man, for example, is what he is through inheritance and the influence of his environment. He has inherited a certain nature from his parents and ancestors, and this nature has been modified in its growth by the external agents which have been brought to bear upon it. Well, according to this philosophy, our present moral dispositions are products of the past. Our philosophers do not make themselves from year to year. They have moral sympathies, moral antipathies, wrought into the tissues of their affections, which do not immediately leave them when they cease to hold the beliefs which made their fathers cleave to good and abhor evil. On their own showing, their present dispositions belong much more to the old convictions than to the new. It has yet to be seen how much toughness of perdurable life a morality divorced from theology, however it may be artificially touched with emotion, will retain in the generations to come.

It is true that the ordinary forces of nature, working in human society, are shown to evolve certain rules of morality. Mr. Herbert Spencer is the great exponent of the ethics of evolution. Man, as he explains, and as every one must admit, has in him by nature a desire to obtain what is agreeable to him. That is the original *nisus* or effort of all animal existence. In acting upon this desire, men have discovered by experience that each by cooperating with others can get more of what he likes than if he stands alone. Hence comes, through mere pressure of natural desire, more and more of association, hence are produced increasingly large and complex forms of society; and as association grows, the sentiments and acts necessary for preserving it grow also. A large society is able to defend its members from injury, which is one of the first requirements of human existence, and to minister to them all kinds of pleasures; but it is upon condition of their helping each other and being true to each other, and therefore of holding severely in check individual desires. The interests of the many transcend the interests of single persons; and common assumptions grow up which have so much force over each separate mind as to bring about the surprising result, that willingness to sacrifice self for others is produced in course of time by love of self. This process, this genesis of social virtue, however paradoxical, is convincingly explained, and must be felt by us all to have a great deal of truth in it. Here, then, it is said, you have nature itself, the most elementary natural desire, guaranteeing social morality; men are made irresistibly unselfish, because each loves himself. We are asked to believe that a progressive morality is secured as a necessity by the fundamental laws of existence. Each person is so interested for his own sake in the well-being of society that the force of the greater number will repress the possible perverseness of individuals, and will train all into the dispositions which promote that well-being. Self-sacrifice will indeed be prevented from going beyond a rational point, as people learn from the naturalist philosophy that social well-being is only an instrumental contrivance for making individuals happy. But each person will find himself under strong pressure to be amiable and considerate, and to make himself agreeable to his neighbours, in order that his neighbours may be induced in turn to make themselves agreeable to him.

This philosophy satisfies Mr. Herbert Spencer and many of his followers. Christians are able, and even bound by their own belief, to accept with reserve its account of progress. We see with interest how the Divine Maker and Instructor has made the happiness of the individual dependent upon the strength and harmony of society, and is training men in social virtues by means of the experimental discovery of what is best for the greater number. The general agreement which actually prevails amongst persons of the most different creeds as to what is really good and praiseworthy is a great comfort to those who reject theology, and is used by them as an argument for the cause of Ethical Culture. There is hope, they say, of complete concord amongst men in the pursuit of justice, temperance, veracity, public spirit; and there is evidently much to be learned about the application of these virtues to conduct; so that the most enlightened may reasonably go to the Ethical Church on Sundays to hear and to be warmed.

But what *authority* has social well-being over the individual? The evolutionist cultivators of ethics tell us that virtue is to be traced to natural desire, and that to be good means to have been pushed to certain feelings and conduct by this universal instinct. Then 'I ought' only means 'the interest of others is making a certain demand upon me.' If you protest, 'To me, my own pleasure is naturally more than the pleasures of others; why should I sacrifice my pleasure to theirs?' the evolutionist may indeed express a doubt whether you are seeking your pleasure in the wisest way, but he has no right to speak to you of your duty. This defect in the evolutionist ethics, the want of power to say 'I ought' and 'You ought,' has drawn out at last a very remarkable protest from that devotee of science and most lucid and candid of thinkers, Mr. Huxley. I say 'at last,' because up to this year Mr. Huxley had seemed to know nothing but evolution, in morals as in the physical world. He has spoken, for example, of a taste for acting virtuously as a chance natural endowment, precisely similar to an ear for music. But in a discourse delivered some months ago at Oxford, which occasioned a good deal of surprise, but of which the significance has not yet been adequately appreciated, Mr. Huxley, knowing well what he was doing, broke away from the evolutionist ethics, put his finger on the defect of which I am speaking, defied the logic of natural science in the region of conduct, and took his place with those who hear a voice of authority bidding man do the right and *not* please himself. If we are to know ourselves only as projectiles of natural desire, then the base and brutal person, Mr. Huxley sees, impelled by his instincts, does not differ in kind from the most virtuous, impelled by theirs; he is no more to be blamed than they are to be praised. Mr. Spencer has managed to shut his eyes persistently to this conclusion of his philosophy, and has been accustomed to denounce wrongdoers with hearty indignation. But Mr. Huxley has now expressed in the firmest words his deliberate and mature conviction that we have a genuine sense of duty, come from whence it may; that we could not do without it; and that the morality which is only that of the cosmic or fleshly instincts has no right to speak of duty.

There are other defects of non-theological morality which are closely allied to—if they are not comprehended under—this principal one. We have been taught to recognise the *inwardness* of our Lord's moral teaching, and the better we understand that teaching the more are we impressed by the thoroughness with which it makes the inward man its object. But the evolutionist morality is pitifully external. It recognises the acts and habits which are most likely to strengthen society; it only treats of dispositions as subsidiary and instrumental to acts. It does not profess to speak to a man's conscience: So far as it addresses itself to a man, it says to him, 'We know that the core of you is appetite and appetite only. You will do the acts which desire, perhaps disguised till it is unrecognisable, prompts you to do. But it will be satisfactory to your neighbours if you will seek your pleasure in ways which will be agreeable to them. If you are too unpleasant to them they will have means of being unpleasant to you. We are sure that in the majority of cases you will get the more pleasure for yourself by accommodating your conduct to your neighbours' pleasure.' I fully admit that all promoters of Ethical Culture will be likely to recognise the necessity of taking character and dispositions into account; but I think I am speaking accurately when I say that the philosophy which understands morality as nothing more than a part of the evolution of desire is contrasted with the ethics of Christ in this respect—that it concerns itself with dispositions, not as in themselves good or bad, praiseworthy or blameworthy, but only as tending to the attainment of the greatest amount of pleasurable existence for so many individuals.

Again, what is a man's nature good for, if it has no reverence? If you could imagine a child entirely without reverence, should you regard such a child with approval or pleasure? It may be said, perhaps, of the philosophy of evolution as a whole, that it directs a sentiment of wonder towards the Force of which the existing universe of things is the result. It is certain that we cannot steadily contemplate the overwhelming greatness of the world and the intricacy of its laws, without a feeling of wonder, which easily becomes a reverent wonder, growing within us. But how is mankind, which we are accustomed to regard as the highest product of the visible world, presented to us by the ethical part of that philosophy?

In order to explain mankind and human history to us, it strips us and our fellow-men bare of all that we have learnt to respect, and exposes us as being at heart merely automata worked by desire. You see a generous and fearless act done, and the emotions it kindles in you tell you what reverence means. Well, when the light of this philosophy is turned upon the act, you learn that your reverence has been but a foolish sentiment. The real nature of the act which has imposed upon you is laid bare. To repeat briefly the steps of the evolutionary argument:—Every man seeks his own pleasure; when many act together, each can get more pleasure; to make united action possible, self must be brought under control; the energy of this politic control of self accumulates in society until the appetite of the more sensitive individuals is cowed, and their imaginations taken captive, by the interest of the many, and so irrational acts of heroism and self-abnegation are generated. This evolutionist interpretation of human conduct not only does not promote reverence—it must tend to chill and quench it. The mind refuses to look with admiring awe upon appetite seeking gratification, when the mask that concealed its features is torn off.

Authority, appealing to the inner man and constraining us to look up to it with reverence—is not this, I ask you, what we chiefly want for our moral life? I doubt whether any of us can imagine ourselves struggling with the difficulties which beset us, resisting the allurements of what we know to be wrong, nerving ourselves in our weakness, bearing discouragement and pain with fortitude, unhelped by the recognition of an authority entitled to our obedience and appealing to the conscience and attracting our better nature to itself.

Between the position of those who believe in natural desire as the one fountain of conduct and that of those who believe in our Lord Jesus Christ, we have to take note of an intermediate position which some at the present moment are attempting to hold. These feel sure there is something that may be called Divine in the universe; they cannot doubt that there are Voices calling them to the higher life of self-control and beneficence: in the mastery won by society over single persons, which to evolutionist ethics is only natural desire being induced by bribes and coercion to stand on its head, they see something like a Divine Purpose training men to nobler and higher conduct: but they are persuaded that we can know nothing definite about the Divine Power, that Christianity—the best of religions—is only one of the pathetic guesses with which human aspirations have thrown themselves out towards the Infinite and Incomprehensible, and that the moral enthusiasms of men are tributes of a blind loyalty to an Influence which may be felt but cannot be seen.

This is a mental attitude which we are bound to treat with the delicacy of sincere respect. You will easily understand the double attraction which it has to sincere speculative minds in relieving them from the obligation to believe in Divine interventions which advanced thought explains as anthropomorphic fancies, and yet saving them from that dogma of self-love governing all things which they reject with an impatience which sometimes reaches disgust. We are passing through a time in which the old conceptions about God and Divine things cannot remain as they were. The view of hopeful faith is, that restrictions are being broken through and errors corrected in order that the belief in Christ and the Father and the Holy Spirit may receive an expansion and elevation which will make Christianity more vital and satisfying and universal than ever. But to some the necessary rejection of traditional notions is enough to send their faith adrift. A cloud receives much more than the visible form of Christ out of their sight, and they stand gazing up into heaven as into a world of mystery and darkness, from which they can only believe that a certain purpose of good is issuing, to blend itself with the consciousness and aims of human life. With reference to this position, to which I allude here as supplying a principle of morals and conduct, I will only observe that the very indefiniteness of view which is attractive to minds in doubt makes the position a difficult one to hold with any definiteness. When we lean on something unseen for support, and ascribe to it authority over ourselves, and claim that it should govern our fellow-men, and try to teach the young to respect it, the Power which we treat thus cannot remain as vague as scientific scepticism prescribes that it should be. The something unknown tends on the one side to receive form or on the other side to become nothing. At present, if people feel themselves constrained to speak of morality as determined from above and not only from below, it will be found that the Christianity which they have inherited and which remains dominant in their ways of thinking, is still supplying them with more of definite conceptions about the supernal Power than they perhaps suppose themselves to be receiving from it.

I have been already in part illustrating the place of Christ in ethics, whilst I have been touching on the doctrines of those who profess to do without Christ in their discussions of the laws of conduct. Let me now speak more directly of what Christ is to Christians in the realm of duty and moral effort.

Christian faith in Christ—that is, in Jesus, the Son of God and Son of Man, who died and rose again from the dead—does not think of Him as a moralist. That is the view of the *non*-Christian admirers of Jesus. These give Him a place by the side of Socrates and Gautama, holding Him to be one of the few who have had the highest ideals of gentleness and goodwill and practical beneficence. But those who believe in the Jesus Christ of the Gospels are not led to think of Him as a teacher of morality. What He professed to give to men, and what He actually gave, was not a code of morals, but Himself.

The view which our Lord took of His own mission may be unmistakably learnt from the Gospel narratives. In His first addresses to His countrymen He proclaimed the Divine Kingdom which the Baptist had previously announced. His teaching was almost entirely about this kingdom. In proclaiming and illustrating the kingdom He spoke of Himself as the Heavenly Father's Son, able as such to declare the Father's mind and purposes. With marked authority He forgave men their sins and invited them to come in faith to Himself and to the Father. But the name which He commonly gave Himself was the Son of Man, and He claimed all men as His brethren. All this is much more characteristic of the Christ of the New Testament and—we may say without fear of contradiction—of Jesus of Nazareth, the living Prophet and Master of disciples, than the delivering of moral precepts. So far as His own conduct was concerned, Jesus let it be seen that He acted and spoke as the Father's Son and the Brother of Men; and the conduct which He prescribed to those who believed in Him was similarly the natural or proper life of children of God and brothers of men.

It is but a poor doctrine of Christian ethics that consents to put the living Christ aside, and endeavours to compile a code of conduct out of His precepts. There are moral precepts of Christ in abundance in the New Testament. The most significant and direct of them are comprised in the Sermon on the Mount, which is generally taken to be the characteristic moral code of the Christianity of Jesus. But when we look at the Sermon, we see that the kingdom of heaven was the real subject of these instructions, no less than it was of the Parables. Our Lord was desirous that His disciples should understand the nature and the demands of the kingdom, and He taught them that in it, whatever they might be doing, they would always be face to face with their Father in heaven. Their aim must be to resemble Him, to please Him, to win His rewards, to avoid incurring His anger. He would know them and deal with them according to their inward actions. This is the main point that our Lord is urging in the Sermon on the Mount, and He puts this spirituality of life in strong contrast with the external righteousness of the Scribes and Pharisees. All through, Jesus is declaring the heavenly Father, and telling His disciples that they must think and feel and act as the Father's children. Similarly, in the places in which St. Paul gives precepts of Christian morality, as in Romans xii. and xiii., he expressly deduces the rules of conduct from the radical principles of the Christian life. Let the mercies of God constrain you to make an offering of your whole selves to God, for the finding out and doing of His will; we are one body in Christ, and severally members one of another; be imitators of God, as beloved children; walk worthily of your Christian calling:—such are the fountains out of which Christian behaviour is to flow. According to the New Testament, status comes first and is all-important, and the life that is to be led by Christians is that which is perceived to be suitable to their status. Christ makes us children of the Eternal

Father and members of a body of which He is Himself the Head, and then invites us to live, to live freely and from within outwards, in the ways in which God's children and the fellow-members of the Divine Society *should* live. In this law of life we have a scheme of ethics contained which is essentially progressive and capable of indefinite development and adjustment. For the Christian, it is to be understood, believes that human society is a Divine creation, and that the design of the Creator is revealing itself in the courses of human history, so that we are to expect constant guidance from the movements going on around us. The ultimate perfection of human life, depending as it does upon the perfection of human society, is not laid down in a code, but is to be discovered and attained through the teaching of circumstances. The constraining authority over us is the will of God; that will we are to study as God's thankful children: and when we wish to know what modes of social conduct we are to call *right*, we may always ask ourselves what will best promote the harmony and health and growth of a body of human beings of which the Christ of the Gospels is the Head. The fundamental principles of Christian ethics are, first, absolute devotion to the God who is building up mankind with loving purpose, and who is such a One as Jesus made known to us; and, secondly, the mind of association with the fellow-members of the ideal human society. These principles leave much to be learnt from experience as to the best modes of conduct; but they keep the Christian always looking to Christ, in loyal allegiance, and in hope of being instructed.

You perceive how much, as regards the *matter* of morality, the Christian will necessarily have in common with all who take the well-being of society as the source of morality. Our loyalty to Christ constrains us to believe that God must will whatever is best for the perfect society. We cannot doubt, also, that whatever our God wills each of His children to do will prove best for the man himself; only we accept Christ's paradox that he who loses himself, not he who loves himself, will in the end save himself. It is open to us, therefore, to associate ourselves in ethical inquiry and effort with those who do not share our faith, without obtruding our theology upon them; but for ourselves, the ultimate authority and the trustworthy guidance for conduct are in Christ. Nor can we imagine any sphere of human action that is not under law to Christ.

Let me illustrate what I have been stating by referring to two departments of conduct about which the minds of the more forward thinkers of our time are especially exercised.

It is always recognised as a characteristic feature of Christian morality that it has from the first laid down so strict and universal a law of *chastity*. It is not the custom of English preachers in these days to expatiate on this subject. We are restrained from doing so, not by any notion that it is obsolete, but by a delicacy more sensitive than has ever prevailed in any other age or is known in any country outside the English-speaking world. I believe that this delicacy, though it may be morbid or fantastic, is one of the genuine products of Christian feeling, and that the observance of it is of greater value as a witness and safeguard than much plain speaking would be. I admit that on this point some think otherwise; it is a question to be decided by the finest instinct and the best-instructed wisdom consulting together. Certainly our Lord spoke plainly, and with his most exacting inwardness, about this branch of conduct; and the Apostles let us see in their writings what a struggle they had in maintaining the high standard of Christian purity against the licentiousness of their time.

As soon as Christ ceases to be acknowledged as the authority over life, nature is ready to assert itself, and the requirement of the Christian law begins to seem too universal or too stringent. M. Renan, for example, writes that, after giving up the Christian faith, he saw that nature does not prescribe chastity. In the book which I have already quoted, which I quote here again because it advocates religious feelings and is of a high moral tone, the author, speaking of the importance 'of recognising that everything moved by the breath of life is sacred and symbolic,' adds, 'In this respect such a book as Whitman's *Leaves of Grass* is more helpful than the New Testament, for it includes more': and Whitman is the American poet who boldly declares, in the name of Nature, that he renounces decency as well as chastity, that he may be like the birds and the beasts. And it is commonly reported that certain French authors, to whom homage has lately been paid as to masters in this country, have written their novels and their poems on these liberal principles.

To believe in Christ is to be taught differently. We have not so learnt Christ. We are bidden to repudiate sternly the dominion of the flesh and of nature. The passions are to have no supremacy in a member of Christ. Christian morality is imperious in the name of Christ on this point. It treats marriage as an obviously Divine ordinance, and prescribes a respectful regard towards all the rules concerning the relations of the sexes which the society into which a man is born has been led to enact. Such rules are not to be absolute or final to the Christian, but it is his duty to treat them with deference until they are improved. As regards amendment of customs and institutions, there is hardly any limit set by the Christian faith to the action of communities honestly seeking improvement, even when they deal with things so fundamental and vital as the relations between the sexes. The one unalterable decree of Christian morality is that individual passion is *not* to claim to do what it likes, that Nature shall *not* be recognised as the mistress of human conduct.

The other duty on which I desire to say a few words is that of observing justice. You may perhaps have tried, not very successfully, to explain to yourselves what justice is by the definitions commonly given of it. To a very large extent, indeed, the justice with which we are all concerned is a simple matter—the observance and enforcement of the law of the land. But justice is invoked by social reformers in behalf of *amendments* of the law, and also in matters which are left by the law to voluntary arrangement. It may look satisfactory to explain justice as the giving to each of that which is his own

—until you ask, what *is* a man's own? If you say, with regard to the question of wages, justice requires that labour should have its due share of what it produces, you may touch a chord of sentiment, but you will perceive that it is no explanation of justice to lay down that it consists in assigning to every one what it is just that he should have. Now, the idea of justice—for righteousness and justice are two words for the same thing and for one Greek word—is very closely associated in the New Testament with the Lord Jesus Christ. He is the Just One; He came expressly to make known, whilst He was visible on the earth and afterwards through the ages, the name of the Just Father. God is righteous or just, in being the Fountain of order, of that order or system of relations which issues from His creative will throughout the creation. The spiritual relations between spiritual beings form the highest part of the universal order. As Christians believe, the fundamental relations of human beings are revealed in Christ; they are those of sonship towards God, and fellow-membership in the social body of which the Son of God is the Head. But this spiritual order in which God adjusts human beings together, and the fulfilment of which is the righteousness of the world, is a struggling and progressive order. The Divine energy is pressing us forward, towards higher and higher social ideals—ideals which reveal themselves to sensitive and aspiring souls through their contemplations of perfect sonship and perfect membership. The order which thus beckons us onward is the ideal justice of the time. The old order, fixed in the laws and conventions of the existing society, is of an importance which the zeal of reformers is apt to underestimate. Without the law of the land, regulating possession and keeping the peace, what would become of us? Read about other ages and other countries, to learn of what inestimable value law, acquiesced in by the population and properly enforced, is in giving us the trust, the quietness and confidence, the power of forming and carrying out plans, which are the fruit of righteousness in a society. And the ideal policy for a community is to feel after new adjustments which will develop yet further its happiness and spiritual wealth, without any such violent changes as would disturb trust and discourage calculating forethought.

The prevailing hopes of the present time are set upon improvements in the condition of the labouring classes. Our world is manifestly made the better, the more agreeable to the Divine will, by the improvements which have taken place within living memory in the circumstances and the life of those classes;

and the movement is still going on, and with ever-increasing momentum. It will be agreed, I think, that what the working classes need for their elevation, even more than a greater command of comforts and advantages, is stability of employment. A gradual rise of wages and increased security of employment—these two conditions would be features of a better order, forms of a higher development of justice, in our community: and that is the way in which the principle of justice, as superior to law and custom, comes into contact with industrial questions. Nothing but confusion is caused by the introduction of the idea of *equality* into social efforts, because harmony, not equality, is the law of the Divine creation, and harmony depends on inequality, and rises in dignity as it grows larger and comprehends greater variety. And what makes the principle of justice so impressive and authoritative to us, and gives such confidence and strength in a struggle to those who are sure that they have justice on their side, is that, either blindly or seeingly, we believe in the better order of the world as having a Divine sanction, and as expressing the will of our Maker—that is, of Him whom Jesus Christ revealed.

To sum up what I have been endeavouring to put before you:—Christ in Ethics is Christ the Son of the

Father and the Head of the Divine body of mankind. Whatever improvement in relations and disposition and conduct has been learnt or can be learnt from social experience the Christian holds himself bound to trace to the Divine Instructor. We are not to stand still in our morality, as those who have received a final infallible code: we are to be as children in this sense also, that we are receiving an education. We meet with difficulties and perplexities as we are making our social way onwards: these we should regard as problems set us to solve, the solution of them depending partly on the use and application of principles which we have learnt to trust, and partly on the close observation and open-eyed study of the circumstances of our time. The Apostle who insisted that faith makes a man what he should be is the same who gave one of the most comprehensive precepts of progressive ethics that was ever penned: 'Finally, brethren, whatsoever things are true, whatsoever things are honest, whatsoever things are just, whatsoever things are pure, whatsoever things are lovely, whatsoever things are of good report; if there be any virtue, and if there be any praise, think on these things.' The Christian is to be always ready to receive what may yet be revealed to him. He who sees with the deepest conviction that Christ *has* proved Himself the

Light of men with regard to life and conduct will look forward most hopefully to new illumination. The grace and truth which came by Jesus Christ will go on doing their blessed work as the supreme reforming forces of the world.

VII

CHRIST IN THE REALM OF POLITICS

'*Open ye the gates, that the righteous nation, which keepeth the truth, may enter in.*'—ISAIAH xxvi. 2.

WE are engaged in making men see that Christ is really Lord of all, not in some vague ideal sense, but actually; that He is supreme in every sphere of human existence. And to-day I speak of the sphere of politics. He is working at this moment to make the nations righteous, as the prophet longed that his own nation should be.

When I say that Christ is reigning, I am expressing a truth which is at once confessed and denied. Every one who believes the Bible must believe in our Lord's declaration to his disciples, 'All power is given unto Me in Heaven and in earth.' Every man who repeats the Creed declares that Christ is sitting at the right hand of God, which means that, as the king's chief minister was placed at his right hand in Oriental courts, so Jesus Christ is the Chief Ruler in the

Kingdom of God. But the very people who acknowledge this with their lips are apt to start back when you tell them that Christ is ruling in the sphere of politics; that He is making the laws, deciding the elections, guiding the cabinet council or the parliament; that He acts through the judges and the administrators of the affairs of the realm. I have, therefore, a hard task to convince my hearers that this is true.

I will begin by a statement which may clear away many difficulties. It may be objected to me that politics are very often quite unchristian—that men engage in them from selfish motives, and conduct them with violence or favour or partisanship. If Christ is reigning, they say, why does He not at once put an end to all this and make the national life completely pure? I answer by quoting His own words. He was asked by Pilate if He was really a King? and no doubt the haughty Roman was moved half to laughter, half to scorn, to think that the peasant-criminal before him should pretend to be a King; for he thought, as many Christians now think, that, if He were King, He would exert His power at once and sweep away all that opposed Him. But His answer makes things clear. He vindicates His royalty absolutely; but He declares that it consists, not in a force which would make His will outwardly and at once supreme, but in the convincing power of truth. 'A King! Ay, indeed; for I came into the world to bear witness to the truth; and all who are true men become My subjects.' This is the true royalty: the power to convince men and win their allegiance to the truth. This, and this alone, is the power by which Christ asserts His dominion.

It follows from this that the process is slow. If it were a question of conquest with the sword, a few sharp blows would accomplish it. But the kingdom which is not of this world (although it has its first development in the world) must make its way gradually, by the force of truth. Truth rarely asserts itself suddenly. If it did, it would very likely produce but a weak and transitory conviction. Even where it flashes suddenly on the mind, it needs to be proved by action before it fully lays hold. It comes by reason, by the force of events, by trials and disillusionings, by long experience. Its seed grows secretly, while men rise and sleep night and day, till at last it bears its fruit. And this is eminently the case with social truth, which is above all a truth of experience. Some mathematical or physical truths may be demonstrated once for all; but what belongs to man's social nature is complex and difficult to apprehend, and needs long effort to reduce to practice.

It is thus that we affirm that Christ reigns though His kingdom come in but slowly. The true principle makes its way, but it is a light shining in darkness, and the darkness is only by degrees expelled.

What do we mean by Politics? We mean the science of the people's good: the science which teaches how a nation may be built up to its noblest ideal; how classes within it may come to have right relations one to the other; how its laws may be, like those of Israel, laws of God because they are a reflexion of His righteousness; how in the making of these laws the interests of all classes may be recognised, and in their administration impartial justice may preside. St. John says that Jesus died for the Jewish nation; and it is not too much to say that He laid down His life for political justice, to produce not only good men but good nations. The gates which are lifted up for the King of Glory to come in, are to be opened not only to each redeemed soul, but that the righteous nation which keepeth the truth may enter in.

I affirm that this process of bringing in political righteousness has been going on in the past, is going on now, and is to go on in the future, till the whole social state of all the nations of mankind is thoroughly pervaded by the Spirit of Christ.

(1) I look to the past. Christ as the Word of God, so St. John bids us believe, was guiding the human race before He appeared in the flesh. When good men, whether in Israel, or in China, in Greece, or Rome—Moses, or Confucius, or Zoroaster, or Manu, or Solon, or Lycurgus, or Numa—sought to do justice among their fellows, Christ was there. When Plato sought for righteousness written in big letters in the life of a just commonwealth; when Aristotle showed that though the State might be formed by the necessities of life, yet it was bound to seek for righteousness, and that though men came together to *live*, yet they were together to *live well*,— Christ was there. When the law of Israel gave rights to the slave and the debtor, and bade the judges execute impartial justice between all classes aright, and even called them gods because they did such divine work; when it bade the rich leave part of their harvest for the poor; or when the prophet Isaiah drew the picture of the ideal ruler as one who would judge the poor with righteousness, and reprove with equity for the meek of the earth,—Christ was there. But He was there as a power working unconsciously in men's minds. It is since His incarnation that we see His work most clearly, and realise its full power.

In the little Christian communities of the first two

centuries men tried to live out a perfect life in all their relations; the Christian impulse which made the earliest believers give up their property readily for the good of the whole body coloured very largely the general life, and imbued their discipline with the spirit of self-renouncing love. When the Empire became nominally Christian, this spirit of love and righteousness left a distinct trace upon the laws of the great Emperors, Constantine and Theodosius and Justinian. Later on the penitential discipline of the Western Churches gave a model for law which has only in quite modern times been recognised, for it looked always to the reformation of the wrongdoer. And all through the Dark Ages a process was going on by which the social and political state of mankind was gradually undergoing the influence of Christian principles. Out of the formless chaos of barbarism Christendom gradually was evolved: orderly nations were formed where hordes of unruly beings had wrought rapine and violence; slaves were emancipated, women were raised, war was mitigated by chivalry, the violence of kings was curbed by great churchmen and by peers, the unruly barons were tamed by the national power, the justiciary took the place of the man whose only law was his own will, and lust and violence were stayed as offences 'against the peace of our Lord the King.' Even in those rude ages we may trace the rule of Christ making itself felt more and more.

But how much more has this been the case in modern times, since the truth contained in the Bible was unchained, and men learned once more that they were sons of God, and dared to act as directly responsible to their Father in Heaven! Wars there have been, but how much less savage! How much the consciousness of human brotherhood has checked the hatred of race and the lust of dominion! How great has been the progress of knowledge and general enlightenment! How largely the lot of the weaker classes of society has been ameliorated!

I would take as a special instance the political progress of our own country. What we call the British Constitution is, to speak generally, nothing else than the effect of Christian righteousness, of mutual considerateness, working on the public relations of men. When you see the power of the Sovereign subjecting itself to that of the nation, when you see the franchise given to class after class, what is the meaning of this, but that we have come to desire and determine that no class shall be treated unjustly, but that all should have the opportunity of stating their wishes and demanding redress for their wrongs—that the laws should be made not in the interest of a few but of all? The effect of this in the promotion of political justice may easily be shown.

Take the case of Free Trade, in which our country has led the van. What does it mean but that we will not, for the advantage of a few great men, whether landowners or manufacturers, tax the hard-gotten gains of the masses. Sir Robert Peel, when he abolished the tax on corn which inflicted such hardship on the people, quoted the words of the petition for Parliament in our Prayer Book, and said, 'I have sought to build up peace and happiness on the foundations of truth and justice; and,' he added, 'I shall leave a name remembered perhaps at times in the dwellings of the poor, when they shall refresh themselves after their toil with abundant and untaxed food, the sweeter because it is no longer leavened with injustice.' Was not Christ the Righteous King making his influence felt in the great event which gave occasion to these eloquent words? And what can be said of such public acts as the reform of the prisons, the abrogation of the harsh penal laws which hanged a man for stealing a sheep or transported him for the theft of five shillings, and the recognition of the principle that not the safety of the community but the reformation of the offender should be the main object of punishment? What of the foundation of Reformatories and Industrial Schools, which try to prevent children and young criminals from sinking into perdition? What of the Factory Acts, which protect women and children from excessive toil? and the Education Acts, which ensure to every child now free instruction in the rudiments of knowledge? One by one the fetters on knowledge, on industry, on combinations of workmen for mutual advantage, have been shaken off: and the process by which all this has been done has, we may be sure, been due to the influence and the Spirit of Him who laid down His life for men, and now is reigning to succour them.

(2) Thus far we have dealt with the past: but we must not shrink from carrying on the application of the great truth we are enforcing to the present and the future.

It is very difficult to realise amidst the tumult and cross-currents of the politics of the day the guiding hand of our Saviour. We are conscious of the struggle, and the evils of our present condition often strike us more vividly than any hopes we may have about it. We realise also how mean the motives and actions of men often are. Can we believe that, through all the party spirit, the bigotry, the mistakes, the selfishness of our day, Christ is still by His Spirit working out His own designs, and leading us to righteousness and peace? We often tremble, as we well may, for our country and for the world. But I think that here is the test of our faith: for so it was with the Psalmists; when their feet were well-nigh gone, and their treadings had well-nigh slipped, faith could lay hold of the Providence of God guiding them with His counsel and bringing wickedness to a speedy end.

I take the events of this year which is closing. It has not been very eventful, and some of its records are those of the greatest meanness. France was agitated by the Panama scandals, in which it was found that many of its public men had taken bribes. In America it was found, on the change of Government, that during the last Presidency the public expenses had been increased by something like £30,000,000 a year, simply with a view to keep up a protective system in which all the poor pay for a few rich men. In Germany the resources of the country were being strained to provide more soldiers, more implements of destruction; and all the Continent seemed to be dividing itself into two great camps, in which the Christian nations were deliberately preparing for a war more terrible than any hitherto known. In Italy public frauds were revealed. In Australia dishonest dealing has brought about financial ruin.

That is the evil side. But is there not a brighter one which shows the Christian spirit struggling, and at times prevailing? If there have been frauds, they have been clearly, even relentlessly, exposed to view, and the perpetrators of them have been disgraced. In America the law which required the nation each year to purchase £13,000,000 of useless silver to be hoarded in the Treasury, simply for the advantage of a few possessors of mines, has been repealed, and the removal of other similar evils is promised. If war is constantly apprehended, yet the apprehension grows more and more distant; our French neighbours, whose wish to avenge their disasters constitutes the chief danger, declare that they have no thought of war, but only of self-defence; and this has come out even more strongly since their alliance with Russia, which has ministered to their self-respect while giving guarantees for peace. Above all, we must be thankful that in the Behring Sea Arbitration two great nations have once more settled their differences by peaceful means.

In our own vast possessions abroad two recent events may be hopefully viewed. In South Africa we may trust that the murderous aggressions of the Matabele will cease, and peace and justice reign under our rule: in Central Africa we may believe that the settlement of Uganda has been undertaken, not from vainglory or lust of territory, but in the interests of Christian civilisation. The Opium Commission now sitting may be taken as showing that we are determined not to inflict wrongs upon the people of India and China for the sake of gain, and that, if indeed the traffic is to be maintained by our Government, it will only be so far as it is able to justify it before the eyes of the civilised world.

If we look at home, we scarcely dare to speak of what is being done without fear of partisanship. But I think that any charitable critic will allow that the measures now being pressed on, whether for the separate government of Ireland or for the giving power to the people of each parish to manage their own affairs, or for registration of voters at the public expense, or for vindicating a proper repayment to workmen for injuries they have received, or for giving the people power to save themselves and their families from the ruinous temptations of the drink traffic, are all designed for the Christian object of assisting the weak, even if such a critic should feel grave doubts as to some of the processes by which this end is pursued. The Commissions on labour and on provision for old age are designed in the same interest. The settlement of the coal strike by arbitration is also a testimony to the principle given by Christ Himself (Matt. xviii.) for the composing of disputes, namely, that men should not be judges in their own quarrels, but should bring in other and impartial minds through whom right may be done.

(3) We look on, then, lastly, into the future, and confidently believe that the dominion of righteousness and love will be extended, and the kingdoms of the world become more and more the kingdoms of our God and His Christ.

I have spoken of things which make for peace in Europe. We cannot but believe that the time is coming when Christian nations will look to impartial arbitration as the means of settling their disputes instead of the brutal and unjust arbitrament of battle. We cannot but believe that, in their dealings with the uncivilised or half-civilised peoples, Christian nations will ere long agree among themselves each to take charge of some portion of the task, as has been done in Africa, but to take charge of it not for their own aggrandisement but for the training of the native populations to a higher life. We cannot but believe that such nations as those of India and China will show capacities for a better and stronger life under the Christian influences to which they are being subjected, and that, instead of dragging the world down as some predict, they may come to take a full and special share in its progress.

And, looking at home, we hail the greater interest which is being felt in the social state of the people, and believe that the politics of the future will be mainly concerned with this; so that a politician will in future days come to mean, not one who is trying to make a party prevail for his own advantage, but one who is persuading men in Christ's name to undertake what he believes will promote justice and the good of the people generally: one who will strive for better education, for measures which promote temperance, and social purity, and sanitation, and better dwellings, and thrift, and the co-operation of workmen and those who have been their employers but will become their partners in industry: one who cares for the poor and seeks to diminish the sum of human misery, and who is trying, by harmonising the principles of the conduct of industry by the State with that of individual initiative, to make men at one in the effort for human progress. The greatest question of the future is that between Socialists and Individualists, and we may trust that this will be settled by the acknowledgment of both principles within their respective spheres; for man is both individual and social, and both principles must be at work to build up the perfect man and the perfect society in the image of Christ.

I must conclude. But the conclusion is of the utmost importance, for I seek not only to establish the principle of the supremacy of Christ over politics, but to make you realise that this affects you vitally.

(1) We are coming to see that religion is a matter of the life, not merely of the feelings. If faith in God and in Christ is genuine, it must show itself in every department of our lives. There is nothing secular to the true Christian, but all his actions combine in working out the true man, the true character, the just society of the Kingdom of God.

(2) Every Englishman has to do with politics. We are bound, therefore, to use our political power in God's service, that all our public life may be just, loving, holy, and our nation may be as a temple of the righteous God.

(3) If this is to be done, it must, like all Christian acts, be a matter of earnest, loving labour; no light casting of a vote here, attending a meeting there, or

joining in a thoughtless cry, but sober, steady work for political good; it must mean a real sympathy with others, especially with those weaker or poorer than ourselves; and it must mean a readiness to deny ourselves, to take a lower social place, if thereby others can be benefited, after the example of Christ, 'Who, though He was rich, yet for our sakes became poor, that we through His poverty might be rich.'

(4) We need, lastly, the firm conviction of that which is the keynote of all these sermons, that Christ is veritably the King and Lord, the supreme moral power in the universe. Let us hold this fast, and it will enable us to persevere, to carry our Christian principles into public life, to choose the right, the noble side in each question, till the number of faithful workers grows greater than those that oppose them, and the evils we strive against be cast down, and the life of England and of the world grows instinct with the energy of the righteous God.

VIII

CHRIST IN THE REALM OF SCIENCE

'*So is the Kingdom of God, as if a man should cast seed upon the earth; and should sleep and rise night and day, and the seed should spring up and grow, he knoweth not how. The earth beareth fruit of herself; first the blade, then the ear, then the full corn in the ear.*'—ST. MARK iv. 26-28.

I DOUBT whether the Christian Church at large has appreciated the force of Christ's parable-teaching. As elsewhere, the letter has killed the spirit. In seeking out the revelations in the individual parables men have forgotten the revelation of the whole. That revelation is briefly that besides the written Book which comes to us through human channels, there is another Book in God's own handwriting, the Book of Nature, which we must study. When Christ would explain God's way of working, He describes the growth of the seed, the spread of the leaven; He appeals for proof to the sunshine and the rain, the birds and the flowers. Or, again, in a problem of moral duty He solves the question by the story of the Good Samaritan, the Unmerciful Servant, the Unjust Steward, and the like. He says in effect, 'Do you want to know what God will do with men? See what He does in nature, in the material world.' 'Do you want to know how to act as God would have you act? Learn your duty by studying man's action towards his fellows.' In the two volumes of this great book, the Book of Nature and the Book of Human Nature, you will find the revelation. You will remember that He appeals comparatively seldom to the Scriptures for the sanction of His teaching. He quotes the letter of Scripture to enlarge it, as in the Sermon on the Mount. He quotes the Mosaic law of divorce to show that it was neither original nor final. In speaking of Christ as King in the realm of Science it is necessary to make these preliminary remarks. We need to remind ourselves that He bases His teaching on the assent of the educated reason, not on mere authority. (I say, of educated reason, because nothing can be more contrary to His teaching than the solution of such questions by what men call common sense.) In the passage usually quoted to establish the value of authority—'The scribes sit in Moses' seat; all things therefore whatsoever they bid you, these do and observe'—He throws on them the responsibility of private judgment by adding, 'but do not ye after these works.' Further, in His remarks on Corban, He shows that the command to obey their teaching is limited in application. Even when He speaks with authority as the Son of God, He enforces His teaching by an appeal designed to win their assent—' That ye may be as the children of your Father which is in Heaven.' When He reverses the traditional law He uses the precedent of their own instinctive acts. The Sabbath law cannot be retained in the rigour of the letter, because they instinctively disobey it in watering their flocks; because the priests necessarily disregard it in ministering to the people; because David, rising to the spirit of the apothegm, 'I will have mercy and not sacrifice,' travels on the Sabbath, and eats the shewbread, which is lawful for the priests only. He came to establish the Kingdom of God. When He wishes to describe it, He usually begins 'The Kingdom of God is like,' and then He draws some picture from one of the two volumes of the Book of Nature. Science in the same way bases the conclusions which it establishes on the observation of phenomena, and an appeal to the educated reason. It creates a working hypothesis to explain the difficulties which need solution. When by an exhaustive process of observation and experiment it has proved that this hypothesis meets the objections which can be urged against it, it demands our assent to the theory. In the same way difficulties which meet us in religion are to be interpreted not by Scripture only, not by an appeal to authority, not by Scripture as interpreted by antiquity—but by Scripture illustrated by natural facts, by an appeal to a reason educated by a study of these, in a spirit of reverence and humility, waiting on God for the light needed.

It falls to my lot to-day to speak of the light thrown by science on religion: to ask how far it establishes the teaching of Christ. I shall confine myself to one branch of discovery, the law of Evolution. I shall ask how far this teaching is consistent with, how far it illustrates, the present and future of that Kingdom of God which was the main subject of our Lord's deliverances. Christ taught us that the world was under the governance of God; that He designs to bring it more completely under His rule. His Kingdom is, He says, to dominate the world. Meek, and contemplating in the present much failure, He yet never falters as to the ultimate future of the Kingdom, or in His assertion of His own Kingship. Men are members of that Kingdom, and when they realise their position the world will be a very different place. He does not attempt to prove the existence of God, or that the invisible things are the only things which are real and permanent. This He assumes, and prophesies the ultimate victory of the spiritual over the material—the ultimate victory, for He ever describes the process as gradual. There is this in common between the teaching of Christ and the teaching of Science, besides that appeal to educated reason of which we have spoken: both speak of progress. The scientific man, limiting himself to facts, speaks mainly of progress in the past; Christ deals with progress mainly as regards the future. If I can at all establish the points which I wish to make, I shall show you that the facts of Evolution help us to realise the truth of His prediction, and throw great light on the difficulties which encumber our reception of it. I speak not as a scientific man, but as one who hopes that the aid which science has given to him in the study of morals may be useful to others. What then is Evolution? The world is divided into two spheres, organic and inorganic—matter produced, and matter which has the power of reproducing itself— lifeless and living matter. As regards inorganic matter, it has been the discovery of this century that it was developed not by revolution but by evolution. The theory once was that successive epochs of creation and destruction had by violent action created the mountain ranges, contorted the strata, carved out the valleys. We have learnt that, built up in successive orders of architecture, the temple of creation wears the form it now presents. Science, calling to aid the services of the astronomer, the geologist, and the traveller, has shown us that the forces which now shape the earth were sufficient to build it. Astronomy shows us worlds forming out of star-mist, the geologist traces the evidence of similar action, the traveller shows us the forces still in operation. We come by research to the conclusion that the centre of the earth is still a molten mass; that the crust of the earth is elastic as a sheet of ice; that pressure upon one part, due to the shrinkage of the crust as the earth cooled, threw up the mountain ranges and made the valleys. We learn how the ice plough, and the wind chisel, and the rain gouge, and the frost crowbar mould the face of the earth thus modelled. We can prove satisfactorily that the successive formations of the earth have intimate relations one with another—that there is no break in the pedigree of matter. So far the study of inorganic matter leads us. All that we see was developed out of previous forms by slow and gradual processes, which are still in action. How and when matter came into the world we know not.

Similarly the study of organic matter brings us to a like conclusion. There have not been, as once was supposed, continual successions of activity and repose on the part of the creating power. Life once developed has grown like the seed—first the blade, then the ear, then the full corn in the ear. The unrolling of the genealogy of life shows no gaps. The story tells us not of the destruction of one order, or the creation of a new one.[1] There has been a gradual development of life, one form passing into the other—protoplasm at the base, man at the top of creation. That there had been a development of organic as of inorganic life, taking higher and still higher forms, was known to geologists. It remained for Darwin and Wallace, thirty-five years ago, to do for organic matter what Lyall and Hutton had done for inorganic, to trace the connection between the successive stages, and show us the processes still at work. How and when life came into the world we know not. A short account of the development of life by evolution must be given. It is noticed that no two things which have life are exactly the same. You can find no two leaves which exactly cover each other, no two ears with the same convolution, no two voices which have the same

[1] Thirty, and sometimes sixty, per cent. of forms in one geological period survive in the next.

compass. Nature seems to be ever trying experiments. Variation is a condition of life, and if we were to use the language of teleology we should say that these variations arose out of a desire to produce something better. Two laws govern the existence of variation: adaptation and heredity. Adaptation: if the variation enables the organism better to maintain existence in the surroundings in which it finds itself, better, that is, than the companions with which it is associated, the variation becomes permanent. Then by the law of heredity which allows parents to communicate peculiarities to their children, it is handed down as a legacy to posterity. Evolution shows us these laws at work, and traces the method by which one species passes into another, how organs are gradually developed, how the lower form passes into the higher. Two subordinate processes establish the facts: atavism and embryonism. Atavism, sometimes called hysterology, is a process of deterioration. Everything has a tendency to hark back to the condition whence it sprung: the garden flower to become wild, animals to lose distinctive peculiarities, man to become a brute. Further, the study of embryology, the process by which all things pass in the higher orders to full life, shows us that the undeveloped fœtus takes forms belonging to the lower order, and eventually discards them. In Darwin's *Descent of Man* you will see how this is applied to the establishment of a truth which has been considered degrading to the Lord of Creation. The ultimate fact or factor which rules the whole activity of nature in adaptation and heredity is named the struggle for existence. The population is relatively in each individual part of the world too big for it. This is true whether the organism is fighting to establish itself, or whether it has culminated so far as the organism under consideration is concerned. Relatively, not absolutely, the world is too narrow for every living thing. Each thing like each man tries to make better terms for itself. In the fierce struggle to maintain itself the organism develops new powers, powers superior to those which the predecessors possessed. In this struggle there is often the prophecy of a future which waits long for realisation. When the victory is won the organism bears traces of developments no longer useful. It remains to add that the result of the struggle is described in the term 'the survival of the fittest.' Not the biggest, not those creatures which look strongest, win the day. The huge fauna and flora of the geological ages have given place to a vegetation and race of creatures which are relatively insignificant in appearance. Man is a feeble creature when compared with many of the animals; but he is the lord of creation, surviving because he is the fittest to survive, and still retaining in fable and legend the memory of the struggle which his prehistoric ancestors endured, conquering not by might, but by power of mind.

Now, before we pass on to see what light this theory casts on the gospel prediction, let us very briefly note the parallel in history, the story of man. At a certain time the struggle for existence ceased to produce any higher material form. The battle was thenceforth carried on in the moral world, or at least with weapons directed by other than material force. In dealing with organic and inorganic nature, we have had to trust to the inquiries of the men of science. In this department we can examine for ourselves. It needs no depth of study to recognise the parallel in human thought and action. Man must, if he will live, be constantly changing. These changes, apparently at times mere whims, are seen, when examined in the whole field of life, to be attempts to adapt himself better to existence or to get better terms for himself. The variations sometimes die stillborn; if they become constant, they are transmitted to his children, his family, his race. In the progression of the most progressive there is deterioration which calls out the groans of the moralist, the sighs of the philanthropist. In the upward struggle you have but to scratch the Russian to find the Tartar. Each general movement has begun with a prophet whose voice was as one crying in the wilderness. The prophet has had his successor in a time when the conditions gave his message power to live. The idea takes possession of the nation; it becomes a possession of the world. The land is none the less studded with the statues and the tombs of the apostles, the heroes, the saints, who were once, as inventors, innovators, and martyrs, ridiculed, execrated, and executed. In the fierce struggle which established the victory of truth, there are developed moral qualities which must outlast the inventions, the improvements, the special form of truth—courage, and patience, and faith. 'We live by admiration, hope, and love.'

One more pause to review our conclusions. We postulated a time when there was no matter; we postulated a time when there was no life; we postulated a time when the moral life began. No man has yet bridged the gulf between organic and inorganic life. If there was a time when matter was star-mist, and a time when star-mist did not exist, we might naturally presuppose a time when life was not, and when the inner life was yet unborn. If the evolutionist succeeds in establishing the fact of

L

spontaneous generation, our deductions will have so far to be recast. If the other gulfs should ever be bridged, our hypothesis may have to be altered, but the conclusions will remain much the same. They seem to me to postulate a Creator. Given matter, it takes higher and still higher forms, *i.e.* forms producing conditions in which the highest form of matter, organic life, can exist. But as to the origin of organic life, and how it was engendered, science is silent. Given organic life, it proceeds in successive stages till man stands on the scene in the image of God. But here is a second hiatus. You can find adumbrations of organic life, may be, in inorganic life. At least, sound and form are common to both. You may find prophecies of the higher life in animals; the organ which is to be the seat of the higher life may be developed, but between the highest animal and the lowest man there is an immeasurable distance. The scientific man has no explanation for these breaks, these gaps in evolution. We explain them by the existence of a creative mind, and recognise a Creator at work in the epochs which lie between the gaps. The old theory of teleology has, however, been modified. We no longer believe in a Creator who moulded every living thing. We believe in a Creator who works by law. Paley's illustration of the watch has to be modified. It is as if in the use of that illustration we should conceive of an invention, passing the bounds of imagination, and making a watch which could create a repeater or a clock. We hold to the illustration so far as it helps to register the fact of a Creator; we enlarge the conception to illustrate what we have learnt of His methods.

We come at last to consider how far the message of evolution tallies with the predictions of Christ. He does not argue about the invisible world: He assumes it. On the assumption He bases a prediction as to the future. He assumes that man's reason will assent to the dictum, 'a man's life consisteth not in the abundance of the things that he possesseth,' that man will, when the conception is put before him, rise to it, and 'labour not for the meat that perisheth.' He predicts a future when this shall be accepted, when the Kingdom of God shall be established on the earth, and men shall no longer obey the dictates of the senses. If you have followed me thus far, it seems to me that evolution gives the strongest support to His prophecy. In the grand faith of the great Apostle of the Gentiles, all creation is seen groaning under the struggle towards a higher life, and his faith reads those groans not as the cries of the death-throe—they are the travail of the new birth. If we cast our eyes back on the past, it seems impossible that things can remain as they are. It is only the sense-blinded who cry out, 'Where is the promise of His coming, for since the fathers fell asleep all things remain as they were?' A creation in which matter has come into existence, a creation into which organic life has entered, a creation in which the Darwinian struggle for existence is no longer mainly concerned with the material life, in which thought is the true strength and aspiration the real life—must have a future. Can creation stop here? Does not evolution postulate a still further development? Are not the aspirations of man the prophecy of the future? If this were the best of worlds, would not man, the best of creations, be satisfied with it? Humanity is struggling like Rachel's twins in the womb of futurity. The firstborn is a man of the flesh—Esau; the second which follows is Israel—the Prince of God.

Consider what light the facts we know as regards the struggle of which evolution tells us cast on the higher life. The higher life begins with a belief in God. One of the great difficulties in the belief arises from the existence of disorder and discomfort in the world, the existence of evil, and the slow victory of truth and righteousness. Now, if evolution had shown us any period in which the conditions of life were better than they now are, we might despond and doubt. But if it has shown us that progress is the law which governs creation, that each creation was good, very good for the time in which the verdict was passed: good relatively to the conditions of the present, good relatively to the vanished past, but good always giving place to better, which was still only good, not perfect—why should we trouble ourselves about present imperfections? We are simply imagining a Creator after our own human conception, and quarrelling with Him that He does not make the world as we should have made it. Let it be enough for us that we have found in creation that the race has not been to the swift nor the battle to the strong, and that history confirms the verdict and shows us, despite the backwaters in the stream of progress, the general victory of truth over force, of right over strength. We know not why the struggle is necessary, but we see in the struggle the development of qualities which are cheaply purchased at the expense of it. The world seems to some with imperfect vision a shambles, a surgery. But if in the struggle to which the reddening tooth and the ravening claws bear witness, of which the battlefield and the explosion tell, there is much to puzzle us, we may surely, if we follow the Divine Surgeon at His work, take heart. We shall see that He inflicts pain only to preserve, and to better life. The ghastly details of a battlefield are terrible reading, the story of a colliery explosion is a trial to faith. Turn the page. There are stories of self-sacrifice and heroism which make the heart beat fast and the tears well out in the voice which recounts them. The wards of a hospital are a bigger trial to faith than any dogma of the theologian; but if we could preserve all the wealth of sympathy and tenderness, of skill and courage, which the pains of the sufferer call out; if we could weigh in a balance the results in the development of character and the growth of a deeper life which these scenes have produced; methinks we should cease to pass hasty judgment on the action of the Creator. 'Lord, if Thou hadst been here, my brother had not died,' we cry out in our impatience at the existence of evil. His quiet answer is, 'Said I not that, if thou wouldest believe, thou shouldest see the glory of God?'

The slow progress of truth and right in ourselves and in the world is another of the puzzles. If the Creator designs to bring on victory, why is His chariot so long in coming? Why tarry the wheels of His chariot? It is a truth in evolution that nothing maintains existence till the conditions are such as to permit of the development. Generally speaking, in proportion to the slowness of the development is the strength and vitality of the production. The waste of time is only apparent. There are many prophecies of matter which are like the words of the prophet in the wilderness, which never seem to come to pass. But the prophet's voice, lost in the wilderness, re-echoes in the everlasting hills, till at last it strikes man's attention. Take a simple illustration of the apparent waste from the world of matter. The gigantic creation of the coal measures taxes our imagination to the utmost strain. For centuries they grew, and then for countless ages were buried fathoms deep in earth. Ages rolled on, and when man was in a condition to avail himself of the creations of those ages, these products banked at compound interest see the light, and the splendid activity of the nineteenth century commerce is set to work. There is no waste: the sunshine of the past ages becomes the motive power of our machinery. In all manufacture the process of disintegration, involving much apparent waste, precedes the process of recombination in a new and better form. The delay at which we murmur, and the destruction over which we sigh, are but the means to an end far greater than we could have imagined. We are puzzled with the method, but the result never fails to justify the great Artificer. If, then, Christ prophesies of a future in which the kingdoms of this world shall become the kingdoms of our God, and He shall reign over all and in all, we have in our impatience only to digest His saying, 'Mine hour is not yet come.' In the time He has chosen the miracle will be worked, and His glory shall be manifested.

Perhaps the hardest of trials to faith is the waste of life, and the uncertainty as to the future when the life which means so much to us is over. As to the waste of life: so many seeds sown, so few fructifying; so many insects born but for the day; so careful of the type she seems, so careless of the single life! The studies of the men of science teach us that there is no real loss in nature—old formations are recreated in a new shape. There is no loss of energy—force dissipated in one form reappears in another. Life destroyed becomes the pabulum of new organisations. As well grumble at the chips of precious marble scattered on the floor of the sculptor's studio (the statue is priceless), as groan over the loss of the lower forms of life when they nourish something greater. The evolutionist who believes in no future must surely accept this statement. Shall we who worship at the Cross of Christ, who are taught that the lesson of self-sacrifice is the grandest exhibition of human energy, that he who saves his life shall lose it, and he that loses his life shall keep it unto life eternal: shall we be disturbed because the lower orders of creation involuntarily compass and participate in that consummation and sacrifice which, when consciously rendered by Him who is above all, makes Heaven ring with the applause of saints and angels? And the future of man! Is man too to be absorbed into some higher form of matter, to find his consummation in a spiritual nirvana? No—a thousand times no. Evolution has taught us that in the progress of life positions are acquired from which there is no retreat. Inorganic matter gives place to organic matter; organic matter perishes not to become inorganic matter, but to form new material in which organic matter may dress itself. When the spirit-life is engendered it makes use of the organic matter as a mantle; and, that mantle worn out, the spirit lives still. Not in the brain, but in the spirit which stimulates the brain, is life. The lower organisms stop short of personality however high they rise. This personality, the expression of spirit-life which makes man long to be immortal, is of the things unseen and eternal, which are of all things most real. The materialist shakes his head. Yet the belief in immortality is older than the theory of evolution, and his discoveries ought to lead him to believe that man's aspirations are prophecies. This belief in immortality found expression in those lines of Euripides which Aristophanes satirised. They may have been imperfect, but they deserved something better than the satire which maybe has preserved them—

> 'Who knows if what we call to live be death,
> And dying life? This only do we know:
> The living suffer ill, but those we 've lost
> Suffer no ill, and no misfortune know.'

To me it seems that the dreams of all the ages find their reality in evolution. It may be still only to some an hypothesis. To the great thinker who tells us of the way in which the hope of immortality struck the first age of men, who lived in a bright anticipation of it as no other age has done, it was a certainty. He protests most strongly against that idea of a material resurrection which has formed the chief obstacle to the reception of the truth. Men postulate as a condition of immortality a physical body identical with our own, and fall into the error which made their ancestors substitute earth-burial for cremation in witness of a corporal resurrection. The Apostle tells us, 'Thou sowest not that body that shall be;' declares in the plainest terms that 'flesh and blood cannot enter into the Kingdom of God;' contrasts the spiritual with the natural as an evolutionist who believed in the spiritual might do, 'howbeit that is not first which is spiritual, but that which is natural, and afterward that which is spiritual.' St. Paul is on our side when we declare that identity is possessed in the soul, not in the body. Given the thought as reasonable, the law of evolution brings strong support to the hope which has never died, nor can die, in the heart of man—the hope of immortality.

A few words in conclusion. It will be said that the idea of creation as illustrated by evolution implies a Creator not omnipotent but limited in power. To me the revelation of evolution is that of the supreme sanctity and beneficence of law. I believe in law—by which I mean a certain set of efficient causes always producing the same effects, so beneficent that I see no difficulty in the idea of an Omnipotent Creator binding Himself by law; because law gives the best conditions for producing certain results. If the whole history of creation bears witness to the fact, how can I disbelieve it? In the future which shall glory in the conception of a God who made all things, instituting law as His vicegerent, I do not fear that the elimination of much which, as miraculous, was once considered to witness to Omnipotence, will tend to a lower conception of the Almighty. Miracle in some sort exists. Again and again, born as out of our time, has been seen an organ, a form, a type which was hereafter to be established. It existed to foreshadow what would hereafter be. It could not develop itself at once, because the environment was not such as to allow it. It was a miracle. Such a miracle was the creation of matter, of life, of spirit. Such a miracle was the advent of the Son of Man. We believe in Christ, Son of Man and Son of God, and, believing in Him, and because we believe in Him, we believe in the miracles of the Incarnation and Resurrection. These miracles are but prophecies of future facts. We are taught to believe that we are partakers of the Divine nature, that we can even now 'sit with Him in heavenly places,' whilst for us is reserved a fuller life, when 'we shall be like Him, because we shall see Him as He is.' If a heathen poet could say, 'We are also His offspring,' why should we disbelieve in that destiny of man which has in all ages been the aspiration of the race in some form?

In all ages, now dimly and now more fully expressed, there has been a conviction that we are by our ancestors connected with God—that we shall live with Him hereafter. The Incarnation and the Resurrection are but the fullest expression of this. Only in Him because in Him dwelt all the fulness of the Godhead bodily, only to Him from His intimate connection with God, was the resurrection then possible. These being facts witnessed incontestably, they become proofs to us that the hope which has gladdened men's hearts as to the future, and stirred him to effort in the present, by dignifying life and immortalising existence, is no visionary hope. That these facts should be revealed in one individual before the time in which they are to be manifestly true of all is in accordance with the teaching of the Book of Nature. I will only add that the greater part of the miracles which the man Jesus performed were miracles of healing, such as men now can perform, since they have so far identified themselves with the Creator as to work with Him by law. When men shall care as much for the moral as they care for the physical well-being of men: when *the* life shall be to them 'not meat and drink, but righteousness, and peace, and joy in the Holy Ghost': then we shall see, as we do see in those who have drunk deep of His Spirit, a development of moral power which shall make the vision of a future life to be shared with Him no longer a mere dream—beyond the conception of an ordinary man. Socrates in his noble allegory of the cave represents men as prisoned here, watching only the shadows of the real things pass before them. We are prisoners of the senses; it is the senses which hide from us that which is real. As Blanco White puts it in his sonnet, we are blinded by appearances:

> 'Mysterious night! When our first parent knew
>   Thee from report divine, and heard thy name,
>   Did he not tremble for this lovely frame,
> This glorious canopy of light and blue?
> Yet 'neath a curtain of translucent dew,
>   Bathed in the rays of the great setting flame,
>   Hesperus with the host of heaven came,
> And, lo! creation widened in man's view.
> Who could have thought such darkness lay concealed
>   Within thy beams, O Sun! or who could find,
> Whilst fly and leaf and insect stood revealed,
>   That to such countless orbs thou mad'st us blind?
> Why do we then shun Death with anxious strife?
> If Light can thus deceive, wherefore not Life?'

It is in the hope that some of the thoughts which I have put before you may help to the rending of the veil of sense, by showing how things within our knowledge suggest developments at present only impossible because invisible to the eye uneducated, that I have presented to you these thoughts on evolution. Science, so far as it limits itself to the discovery of facts, can never contradict God's revelation of Himself in other ways. It may compel us in the future, as it has done in the past, to alter our reading of the meaning of those other revelations. But science exploring the secrets of creation is as true an exponent of God's dealings as theology when it limits itself to one source of revelation. In the *Memoirs of Caroline Fox* we are told that at the meeting of the British Association at York, the date of a coin was under discussion: at last the coin, relieved of an incrustation of dirt, showed the letters D.G. 'So,' said the president, 'does any advance in science reveal to us the glory of God.'

IX

CHRIST IN THE REALM OF SOCIOLOGY

Our grandfathers held slaves, and thought it no wrong. Our fathers before them were lords or serfs; they thought it right that some should command, and no wrong that others should yield up their property, their wills, and their lives.

In our own days the relation between men and men has gone on changing. Employers are no longer justified if they buy labour in the cheapest market. Men are not content with big wages if other men are starving. The principle of leaving every one to himself is giving place to the principle of State interference, and change rapidly succeeds change.

What is the force which drives on these changes? Why did men cease to fight as animals, form a society, and say to one man, 'Be thou our king'? Why did they split up the functions of the king, and make some judges and some teachers? Why did they rebel against the king and cancel his powers? Why did they make laws for themselves, and why are they for ever making new laws?

'That all these changes come about in the struggle for existence' is no adequate answer either to the first question or to the last. It does not explain why the standard of existence has risen; why men who once struggled for means of living now struggle for means of thought and of being.

The answer is incomplete, unless it be added that men have been driven from change to change because they have always been conscious of an ideal manhood, and of a call to make that manhood their own. They have seen in the heaven of their imagination the form of a truer man, and have heard a voice saying, 'This is your life.'

The first man, it has been said, was the animal who became conscious of sin; conscious, that is, of having missed a call to a higher life. The men who fought over the roots of the earth were haunted not only by the fear of death but by a longing for a life of order, and so they chose a king and formed a settled society. The men who owned a king next rebelled, not only because they feared his tyranny but because they dreamed of a life which is peace. The men who make laws and change laws are led on by the belief that men may be just, righteous, temperate, and generous.

The force, or part of the force, which drives men from change to change is the thought of an ideal manhood—the knowledge of a standard of life higher than their own—a belief in the humanity of that power which is shaping their ends, rough-hew them as they may. They dimly feel after a truer manhood, and that it is God's will it should be theirs.

Men have thus age by age pushed upwards, trying by all means to grasp the vision—praying, sacrificing, fighting, and law-making, if only they might live more as they were called to live.

Two or three examples will illustrate my meaning.

The slave-owners of the eighteenth century were more human than the feudal lords of the thirteenth century. They built schools for the poor, founded hospitals, and saved the lives which the feudal lords would have wasted. But they went on buying and selling their negro slaves till slowly a higher standard of life loomed on the horizon. They saw that as long as they kept slaves they must be below that standard, that true men could not profit in the oppression of brother men, and that a slave-owner was degraded by the sufferings and degradation of his slaves. They, therefore, at great cost freed their slaves, and now slavery seems so great a wrong as to justify expense of treasure and of blood in its extermination.

Again, there was much grace and beauty in the French society of the eighteenth century. There was a higher conception of duty in the court of Louis XVI. than in that of Louis IX., even if there was a lower performance. The French nobles of the eighteenth century thought for others as those of the thirteenth could not have thought. But over them the Revolution burst as a deluge. Another standard of human life had made itself clear. In the name of their right to live that life, men fought against privilege, and privilege in the face of that life was powerless.

One more example. Trade a few years ago accepted the law of supply and demand, and left the individual to take care of his own interests. A great development in energy was the consequence. The free man of the nineteenth century—pushing, rough, vigorous, independent—reached a higher standard than that reached by the civil, quiet, and obedient tenant or apprentice of earlier times. But now alongside of the free successful man, under whose feet is a crowd of weaker men who have fallen in the rush, another standard of manhood has become clear. The true man, it is seen, must be pitiful as well as successful, tender as well as vigorous. A system which hampers his development must be changed, and competition is condemned.

In these and in every period when humanity has advanced men have been led on by the vision of the perfect man. A glimpse has been sufficient to make them shake off the fetters of prejudice or tyranny. But in every case the progress has been checked. They who were first moved by this idea of true manhood have come to think it was by some leader or by some system that they have been saved. They have, therefore, ended by trusting in a name or a system, and by thinking that they will go on and on because they are Protestants, Abolitionists, or Republicans. They have not kept their eyes on the form of the perfect man by whom they were first moved, and so the progress has not continued; humanity made free from the fetters of one system has been bound to another system. But step by step progress has been made, and it is this idea of the true manhood—this belief in the humanity of God—this groping towards a higher life as towards that destined for men—which has inspired effort and shaped progress.

This idea, which was always in the world, and may be traced in Jewish, Grecian, and Indian systems, was made flesh in Christ. In Him men's eyes could see and their hands handle the form which had called Abram to leave his father's house to seek righteousness, the Greek to give up gain for beauty, and the Indian to worship sacrifice. In Him, too, economists, revolutionists, socialists see what is the life which they hold to be the right of all men.

Christ is in the world when the world knows Him not. He has inspired its efforts and shaped its progress. His is the gentle voice, soft as the breath of Eden, which has drawn men to love, and His has been the trumpet call which has roused them to strike down their foes. He has broken slavery, tyranny, and neglect. He is the conqueror supreme in all the relations of society. He is the Word of God: the voice of Him whose will is that men should be perfect as their Father is perfect, and whose will must at last be done. The humanity of God has been revealed in His only begotten Son. The Word which was in the beginning has been made flesh and dwelt among men.

There is no need to grope in the past after the ideal manhood, or to ask what is the standard of life. The life of Christ shows what is the life of ideal manhood, and what is the standard of our life. Through Him comes a voice which tells us that God's will is that we should be as He is. 'Put on Christ,' says

St. Paul, 'and you will fulfil all social duties; you will be honest, true, and loving.' 'Let us walk in the light of Christ,' says St. John, 'and we shall have fellowship one with another.' Feed on Christ. 'Take Christ into yourselves.' 'Worship Christ' is but one text of Christian reformers.

It is not enough, however, just to repeat texts or to stir emotions by repetitions of the old, old story. Preachers are sent, as prophets were sent, to be interpreters between the past and the present. They have to declare the Christ of to-day, and show that He who is from the beginning speaks in modern language.

Many Christians take Christ's words as the Pharisees took Moses' words: they worship the letter and miss the spirit. They give their charity and overwork their work-people.

Many look to the Christ of the past and oppose in His name the Christ of the present. They preach of One who went as a lamb to the slaughter, and they condemn Him who rouses men to strive for freedom. They say Christ called men to save themselves, and they refuse to recognise as His the voice in socialism which calls men to give themselves for social needs.

Preachers are sent to declare the Christ of to-day, to translate His Spirit into the modern form, and to direct the world's worship, not to a Jewish or mediæval figure, but to the Son of Man in their midst.

I imagine you as employers or employed asking me about the living wage or the policy of trades-unions—as fathers and sons asking about your rights and duties—as women asking about your position—as Englishmen asking about co-operation, competition, free trade, and socialism—as human beings asking how, with divided interests and divided tastes, you may live as members one of another!

As a preacher I put before you Christ as I conceive Him, interpreting the Christ of all ages into the language of to-day.

In the light of Christ's life, more or less dimly seen, our fathers found a way through their difficulties. In the light of that life more clearly, but still dimly, seen our generation may walk safely amid its dangers.

I preach Christ. I take three aspects of His character: I put Him before you as an Heir, as a Servant, and as a Son.

(1) Christ as an Heir claims the inheritance of the ages. He asks questions of the teachers and inquires of the learned what is the latest discovery. He takes note of all He sees, and knows how the farmer works the land, how the guest behaves at the party, how the steward keeps the accounts, and how the worshipper

is justified. He is careful about what is beautiful. He approves expenditure which has no use but pleasure.

Christ stands out among us a sharp, clear-cut figure, an individual strong in His enjoyment of whatever is good, beautiful, and true.

This is the man all men would be. This is the ideal which draws all men.

As men worship Him they shake off the custom or the prejudice which hinders them from growing to His stature. The long hours of labour which make study impossible, the asceticism which condemns pleasure as wrong, have to be resisted, as well as the self-indulgence which destroys powers of study and enjoyment. Great riches and hereditary titles with their deceitfulness, as well as poverty with its cares of this life, are condemned as hindrances. Prejudices which deny to women the right to think and allow to man the right to sin have to be given up.

Through Christ the Heir a voice reaches every man and every woman compelling them to culture their own being, calling them to study and to work. It forbids the indolence which, in the name of religion or socialism, lets a man depend on others, as it forbids the doles which in the name of charity, or the trade which in the name of political economy, rob others of their independence. It says to each: 'Be active, make yourself healthy, wealthy, wise. Work out your own salvation. Claim your inheritance. Take by force your position as a man able to think, able to enjoy, able to love.'

Christ the Heir beckons His brother in the name of God to come and be as He is. He glorifies individuality.

(2) Christ is a Servant and gives the best. He, by knowledge and by feeling being equal to the highest, gives all for the sake of the lowest. He being lord is servant; He being rich makes Himself poor.

This is, we all say, what we would be. We too would be on earth as those who serve.

Those who worship Him give their best. They who have got knowledge, or wealth, or power, looking to Him, use all for others. Employers with their eyes fixed on Him who served think of their work-people before their profits, and ask in their investments not 'What will the dividend be?' but 'What will be the good to others?' The employed thinking of Christ as he works gives full measure of work, good work, and honest work, and asks, not how long can or may this job last, but how best can time and money be saved.

Christ being in their midst, men do not easily talk of their rights. They do not as capitalists, as workmen, or as churchmen claim anything as a right; they all think first of what they can give, how use their property and their power for the service of the weak, the ignorant, the children, and the criminal.

The Servant in our midst, who is drawing all men to Him, gives everything for others. If we say as the young ruler, 'We have paid high wages, done long hours of work, subscribed largely, and made great sacrifices,' Christ's voice will send us away very sorrowful. We have been keeping the best for ourselves; Christ sanctifies socialism.

(3) Christ is a Son and obeys God's will. He seeks not His own glory and speaks not His own words. He is humble and meek. He comes to do His Father's will, and does, even to the death upon the cross, the work He is sent to do. He stands to-day high above the crowd of leaders who claim credit for themselves, and draws man to Him as to one in whom the weary may rest.

Men as they see Him become ashamed of their aimless lives, as they gather and squander or try to get a press notice of themselves. They feel that man has a mission, and that the true man must be one under authority—strong as one who is the Son of God, gentle as one who has no self to serve.

He who would be as Christ cannot set the glory of

his nation, his class, his scheme before that of his Master, or even for a moment seek the praise of men. Christ strong in God's strength marching unflinchingly to finish the work given Him to do condemns the weakness of the time-server and the servility of every courtier, be it of the crown or of the crowd. He calls on all men to give up their wills and their schemes. He promises them strength, peace, and power as soon as they will say, 'Lo, I come to do Thy will, O Lord.'

Christ the Conqueror is thus among us. His form is clearer, His voice is more searching than in past years. He is gradually drawing nearer, and one day every eye will see Him as He is. He has conquered and He will conquer.

Let us who are in doubt about social right and social wrong take Him as Lord.

Our fathers, who, under His lordship, shook off slavery and tyranny, fell away. They thought it was by their own strength and wisdom they had won. They put their trust in their doctrines of right, in their forms of government or of worship. They forgot that it was Christ, the perfect man, who had inspired, restrained, and purified. They made images of Him in their own likeness. They looked down and not up.

Let us in our day beware of thinking that by our system—our socialism or our individualism—that by our pity or our preaching, we shall do good. Christ is Lord. It is by looking up to Him as He stands in our midst that we shall get power. It is He who will inspire us with new energy and hope. Christianity and social progress cannot be divorced.

Worship Christ, the perfect human, and gradually we shall find that the Power which is above all power is also human, is a Father. Worship Christ, Son of Man and Son of God; we shall know what as men we ought to do, and we shall have strength to do it—the strength to stand alone against the world, and the strength, if need be, to quietly give ourselves that others may rise.

X

CHRIST IN THE REALM OF POETRY

'*And an Angel of the Lord stood by them, and the glory of the Lord shone round about them. . . . And suddenly there was with the Angel a multitude of the Heavenly Host praising God.*'—St. Luke ii. 9, 13.

'*Jesus took with Him Peter and John and James, and went up into a mountain to pray. And as He prayed, the fashion of His countenance was altered, and His raiment became white and dazzling. . . . And there came a bright cloud and overshadowed them, and as they entered the cloud they were afraid.*'—St. Luke ix. 28, 34-35.

On any other night than this I think I should have wished to take the second only of these verses as the keyword of what I have to say to you. But to speak of 'Christ in the Realm of Poetry' on a Sunday night, which is also Christmas Eve, I could not well begin elsewhere than here, with these words, which tell of the first of all Christmas carols, the holy song of the angels at the birth of Jesus. For here, surely, in the prelude to St. Luke's Gospel, if anywhere in all the Bible, we are in the Realm of Poetry.

The Incarnation of the Son of Man is the most beautiful of all the manifestations of God. And the story of the Incarnation, as told by St. Luke, is one of idyllic beauty. The Gospel of St. Luke has indeed been well called the Poet's Gospel. It opens with a lyric cry of joy and happiness in the Idyll of Bethlehem. It closes with the solemn, pathetic silence of the Idyll of the Ascension. 'Behold, I bring you good tidings of *great joy*' is the keynote struck by the Angel of the Annunciation on the first Christmas Eve. And as the record begins, so it ends: 'They worshipped Him, and returned to Jerusalem with *great joy*.'

'The whole Gospel'—I quote the words of the Poet-Bishop of our Church—'is like a noble drama, which has a chorus to meet from time to time the splendour or the pathos or the majesty of its development, now wailing, now triumphing; or we seem to be walking in the sacred cloister, not knowing when some hand will "rip up the organ with its thunder stroke," and fill the place with music.'[1]

I regard Poetry as a great gift of vision and utterance bestowed upon humanity in order that life may not be rendered intolerable by the perplex-

[1] *Cf.* Bishop Alexander's *Leading Ideas of the Gospel*, p. 140.

ing enigmas of the universe, by the horrid practicalities of everyday humdrum existence; that the hopefulness of the race may from time to time be made sure by the perception of a divine harmony pervading the great round of creation. To me, as I say, Poetry is the transfigurator of life. Among the many strange and intricate groups of the tragicomedy of time, Poetry—like Pippa in Browning's lyric—passing, walks the world, singing words whose power she often herself knows not of; and by some indefinable charm, at the sound of her voice, the whole aspect of life changes, evil stands abashed, light looks in on despair, the solution of the dark enigmas of sin and pain and death is flashed upon our hearts:

'God's in His Heaven,
All's right with the world.'

You will not wonder, therefore, that with this conception of the place and mission of the Poet in the world, I should have placed in the list of subjects of this course of sermons that of 'Christ in the Realm of Poetry.'

And I have done so not merely because I believe that the Incarnation of the Son of God has sanctified all human life, and that, therefore, every sphere of human thought and action is a channel, or ought to be a channel, through which the Imperial Christ is acting, and that there is no subject which does not in the end run up into theology, and may be made the vehicle of religious teaching. This is true. But there is more than this in speaking of the Poets as interpreters of Christ in Christianity. I agree, indeed, in this matter with Shelley.

Some of you will remember his words. I have quoted them before from this place. I allude to that magnificent prose fragment of his on 'The Defence of Poetry,' in which he compares the function of the Poet with that of the prophet of old, showing how the latter is in reality the preacher of righteousness rather than the predicter of future events, the man of insight rather than of foresight, the forth-teller of eternal truths rather than the foreteller of things which are to come to pass; and how the inspiration of the true Poet is in fact the same as that of the prophet—there are not two inspirations, for there is but one Holy Spirit—for he too 'not only beholds the present as it is, and discovers those laws according to which present things ought to be ordered, but he beholds the future in the present, and his thoughts are the germs of the flower and fruit of latest time.'

I agree, then, in this matter with Shelley that the

Poets of Christendom are among the true prophets of God in the present dispensation; that it is to their writings rather than to the writings of the theologians that you must go if you would know what real spiritual insight is, if you would feel the true warm religious emotion of men's hearts rather than the cold conventional thoughts of their minds —nay, if you would distinguish often between the religion of Christ and the religion of Christians—in a word, if you would find the Very Christ Himself, as He has been known and worshipped from age to age.

We have not, of course, the time now for the full historical retrospect which would make that position clear. 'The witness of the Poets to Christ' is a subject in itself which would justify a course of many sermons. I must be satisfied, in the time that remains to me to-night, with a much humbler task.

Let me try to illustrate just one aspect of this wide subject by an appeal to three only of the great Christian Poets of our own land. I will take my illustrations from widely different epochs.

It has been, as you know, the underlying thought of all these sermons that Christ is the supreme Personality of all history, the most potent factor of all civilised change and progress. Now, the question I want to ask is this—what witness do the Poets give to that thought? How have the great Poets of England from age to age depicted the supreme Personality of Christ?

It has been said lately by a great religious leader of our day—Principal Fairbairn of Mansfield—that 'the distinctive and determinative element in modern theology is a *new feeling* about Christ.' 'We have,' he said, 'only lately recovered the true historical Christ. We have learned to know Him as no other age has done, as He lived and as He lives in history.'

Well, if this is true—and I believe it is—if we have a *new feeling* about Christ, the question I want to ask is this—What was the feeling about Christ in other ages, in our country's history—in the eighth century, say, or the thirteenth, or the fifteenth? How did it differ from ours? Can the poets tell us?

Let us see. I will ask you to come back with me to the middle of the eighth century.

I.—CYNEWULF.

In the library of Exeter Cathedral there is an old book, or rather a roll of manuscripts, which I have myself seen, known by the name of *The Exeter Book*, containing probably the noblest product of Early English genius. The book has lain in the Cathedral library ever since the day when it was placed there, in the year 1071, by Leofric, the first Bishop of Exeter, the Chancellor of England, the friend and counsellor of Edward the Confessor. In Leofric's catalogue of the books he placed in the library the entry of this book, written in choicest Anglo-Saxon, runs thus: 'A great English book on all sorts of subjects, wrought in verse.' The first place in this book is held by the remarkable poem which is probably the oldest Christiad of modern Europe—Cynewulf's 'Christ.' It is to this poet I would make, then, my first appeal.

Of Cynewulf himself we know very little. He is like Shakespeare, at least in this, that we know less of his life than of his character. His birthplace is a mere matter of surmise. From the fact that the scenery of his poems closely resembles the coast scenery of Northumbria—the storm-lashed cliffs, the wintry tempestuous seas often weltering with ice—it is generally conjectured that he belonged to one or other of the towns of that region—Whitby, Jarrow, Lindisfarne, Tynemouth—all centres of learning in touch with the great monastery school at York, and all places in which a poet would breathe that atmosphere of the sea which is so characteristic of all his poems. Born about the year 715—twenty years or so, that is, before the death of the Venerable Bede, the historian of the early Northern Church—in early life he seems to have been a wandering singer, passing from place to place, 'moving at ease among rich and poor, as ready to verse a rude, even a coarse, song for the peasant or the soldier, as a lay of battle or of ancient wisdom for the ætheling or the abbot or the king; loving praise in the hall and fond of gifts; loving solitude also when the fit came on, and hiding himself from men; having a clear consciousness of his worth as a poet, . . . indifferent to religion.'[1]

Then there came a time when this careless life of the wandering minstrel or saga-singer passed away, 'like the hasting waves'—he says himself—'like the storie which ends in silence.' He is in bitterest sorrow, convinced of sin, fearful of the wrath of God, so full of remorse for the careless past that his song-craft leaves him. He is no more a poet. Then he wins hope again with a vision of the redeeming power of the Cross of Christ, and the craft of song returns. 'God Himself,' he says, 'unlocked the power of poetry in my breast,' and he sings of *The Dream of the Holy Rood, Juliana, Elene, Andreas, Guthlac The Fates of the Apostles*, and *The Christ*.

It is of this last poem that I wish to speak to you. I confess when I read it for the first time in the

---

[1] *Cf.* Stopford Brooke's *Early English Literature*, vol. ii. p. 199.

early part of this year, in the full text which has been lately published by Mr. Golancz, of Cambridge, I was astonished at the lofty sublimity and power of this great Christian epic of the Northern Church in the eighth century, this noble story of our salvation, with its trumpet-tongued passages of joy and piety, its pathetic wailing lyrics of passionate prayer and supplication, its vivid dramatic pictures, its rushing choric outbursts of praise and victory.

The story is divided into three main pieces, dealing respectively with the Nativity of Christ, His Ascension, and the Day of Judgment.

The poem begins with an Invocation to Christ— the King.

> 'Lo! Thou art the wallstone which the workman once
> From the work rejected! Well it Thee becometh
> That Thou hold the headship of this Hall of Glory;
> And the broad-spaced walls of the flint unbreakable
> With a fastening firm fitly knit together;
> That among the earth-burgs all with sight of eyes
> They for ever marvel! Master of Magnificence!
> Now through mighty wisdom manifest thy proper work,
> True-fast and triumphant-clear!'

So the poem begins. Then follows a prayer to Christ as the Ruler and Craftsman of the world, who keeps the keys of life, to have pity upon His people and to save them from the Baleful One, the Scather of Men. The next canto deals with the Virgin Mary and the Birth of Jesus, who as 'the root and offspring of David and the bright and morning star' is invoked in a little lyric which is probably the earliest of English Christmas carols:

> 'Hail, Earendel![1] soothfast and sunbright;
> Sunbeam that enlightenest all the tides of time,
> Come thyself illumine those long since lost in darkness.
> Thanks to the Lord Triumphant that He willed to send
> us Himself.'

The second portion of the poem is taken up with the Ascension and that which followed and preceded it. In this canto there is an episode describing the Harrowing of Hell, closing with a magnificent choric hymn, supposed to be sung by the angels who come forth from the gates of Heaven to meet and welcome the Old Testament saints, as, rising from Hades, they mount the sky with Christ. And then the Christ Himself turns to bid the ascending souls welcome to Heaven in words which might well have been those of an old Norse chieftain to his warriors returning from war with spoils of victory:

> 'Forward now to friends, frankly march along
> With a gladdened heart! O ye gates, unclose!
> He will into you. He of all the Wielder!
> He the King unto His City! He Creation's Lord,
> With no little Army, now will lead His folk
> To the joy of joys.'

---

[1] The supposed name of the Christmas Star.

Then follows a description, in swirling verses full of imaginative splendour, of the Day of Judgment:

> 'Lo, the fire-blast, flaming far, fierce and hungry as a sword,
> Whelms the world withal. Then on every wight
> Fastens the death-flame! On all fowls and beasts
> Fire-swart, or raging warrior, rushes conflagration,
> All the earth along.'

This is followed by the final address of Christ to the good and the evil, the just and the unjust, repeating the whole story of the Fall, the Incarnation, the Crucifixion, the Resurrection. It is full of quick personal appeals, as if Jesus were speaking to one only out of the vast host. There is one specially effective passage on the theme of the Holy Rood. A mighty cross is pictured with its foot standing on Zion's hill, rising till its top reaches the sky. All the hosts of Heaven, angels and men, gaze upon it. By its ruddy light all things are seen. The sun is gone. It shines instead of the sun. It is the brightest of all beacons. All shade is banished by its brilliancy. From head to foot it is red, wet with the blood of the King of Heaven. The good see it and it brings brightness to their souls. The evil see it for their torment and their doom. And in the ruddy light Christ, like a Roman preacher to the crucifix, turns to the mighty Rood, points to Himself hanging there, and cries to the vast host: 'See now the deadly wounds which men have made in My hands and My feet. . . . O how uneven between us two the reckoning! . . . Why didst thou forsake the glorious life I bought for thee through love? Give Me back thy life which I gave thee. I claim the life which thou hast slain with thy sins. Why hast thou crucified Me afresh on the cross of thine hands worse than when of old I hung upon the tree? Methinks this is harder. Thy sins' cross is heavier for Me, bound fast unwillingly, than was that other Rood which once willingly I for thee ascended.'

And so Cynewulf's poem ends with the final locking of Hell and the opening of Heaven to the just, and the description of the Perfect Land:

'There is angel song, there enjoyment by the blest,
There belovèd Presence of the Lord Eternal,
To the blessèd brighter than the beaming of the Sun!
There is love of the beloved, life without the end of death.
. . . Peace all friends between you without enmity.
Love that envieth not . . . but the happy company,
Fairest of all hosts, shall enjoy for aye
Grace of God their King, glory with their Lord.'

How then shall we say that the Personality of the Christ was conceived by this singer and poet of our Northern Church in the England of a thousand years ago?

To Cynewulf, Christ is undoubtedly a Divine and an Imperial Figure, supreme over Heaven and earth, the Lord of glory and the everlasting Son of the Father, the Judge of quick and dead, but yet conceived, surely somewhat saga-fashion, as a victorious King, whose apostles and saints are thegns and æthelings, dispensing gifts of service among His thralls, waging a world-wide war in which Earth and Heaven and Hell are mingled, and who, when the victory over the dark-burg of Hell shall be won, will sit down to feast with His warriors in the Great Hall of the Light-burg of Heaven, amid the singing of the angels, who are the bards of the battle.

Yes, with this once wandering singer the old is still somewhat interwoven with the new. The old Pagan faith is Christianised, but the new Christian faith is somewhat Paganised. And yet Cynewulf's song is a trumpet-voice of the heart which belongs to our English nature; and it is not too much, I think, to say 'that the lofty music of Milton's "mighty-mouthed harmonies," and not less perhaps Milton's sombre Puritan faith and its somewhat lurid conceptions of the future of the unsaved, come down to him in legitimate descent from this earliest exaltation of English Psalm.'

II.—LANGLAND.

Once again, let me ask you to travel with me five centuries further down the highway of time to greet a much homelier figure in William Langland, the Peasant-Poet of the fourteenth century.

His *Vision of Piers the Plowman* covers one of the saddest periods of English history. It expressed the very heart of the English people at the epoch of the Peasant Revolt, that time of social change and upheaval, which yet bore fruit in the emancipation of the great yeoman class, which for three centuries gave so wholesome a stamp to our English national character, and whose subsequent decay is, as I venture to think, the most deplorable event in the later history of our country.

The hero of Langland's *Vision*, Piers or Peterkin the Plowman, is the Ideal Reformer of his time—a poor man, it is true, but then this poet of the people did not forget that in the realm of principles great results are often wrought by humble means. In his poem the grim earnestness of social reformation is tempered continually by thoughts and maxims in which shrewd rustic common sense and broad Hogarthian humour are combined; but always there is the note of social passion, of hearty contempt for hypocrisy, of strong Puritan, almost vindictive, moral fervour.

In the prologue the Poet describes himself as wandering on the Malvern Hills:

> 'I was very forwandered, and went me to rest
> Under a broad bank, by a burnside,
> And as I lay and leaned and looked in the water,
> I slumbered in a sleeping, it sweyved so merry.'

And in his sleep he dreamed, and this was the opening of his dream :

> 'A fair field full of folk found I there between
> Of all manner of men the mean and the rich.
> Working and wandering as the world asketh.
> Some put them to the plough played full seldom
> In setting and in sowing swonken full hard
> And won what masters with gluttony destroy.
> And some put them to pride apparelled them thereafter
> In countenance of clothing come disguised in prayers
>   and penance.
>
> . . . .
>
> And some chose chaffer, they thrive the better
> As it seemeth to our sight that such men thrive.
> And some mirth to make as minstrels conneth,
> And gold with their glee guiltless I believe.'

And some, he says, were

> 'Japers and janglers,
> Judas's children, and some beggars with bags
> Crammed full of bread and druncken and lazy.'

Some were pilgrims and palmers, journeying to Rome, and having 'leave to lie all their life after.' Some weavers and labourers, burgers and bondmen, bishops

and friars, pardoners and parish priests. Of these,
alas! he has little good to say :

> ' Parsons and parish priests plained them to the bishop
> That their parishes were poor since the pestilence time.
> To have licence and leave at London to dwell
> And sing there for simony, for silver is sweet.'

But whoever the people were of whom our dreamer
dreamt, it is plain that they were all the people of this
everyday waking world. And all these, he goes on
to tell, were bidden by the fair lady, Holy Church, to
take up the Quest of Truth:

> ' A thousand of men there thronged together,
> Cried upward to Christ and to His clean Mother
> To have grace to go with them, Truth to seek.'

On failure, however, of any to guide them on their
road, Peterkin himself offers to be their leader :

> 'By S. Peter of Rome, he cries,
> I have an half-acre to ear by the highway.
> Had I eared this half-acre and sowed it after
> I would wend with you and the way teach.'

But Truth himself appears to the Plowman, and tells
him that the work of ploughing and sowing his half-
acre is so important that he is not to leave it, even to
lead a pilgrimage. The aim of the Plowman is to
work, and to make the world work with him. If all
good men go on pilgrimage, who is to do the world's
work ? So Peterkin stays at home and preaches the

Gospel of Work and Brotherhood for Christ's sake. And this is how he preaches it. 'Christ,' he says,

> 'Gave each man a grace to guide himself with,
> That idleness encumber him not, envy nor pride.
> Some He gave wit with words to show,
> Wit to win their livelihood with as the world asketh;
> As preachers and priests and prentices of law
> They loyally to live by labour of tongue,
> And by wit to make wise others as grace them would teach.
>
> . . . . .
>
> And some He learned craft and cunning of sight,
> With selling and buying their livelihood to gain;
> And some he learned to labour a loyal life and a true;
> And some he taught to till, to ditch and to thatch;
> And some to divine and divide, numbers to know;
> And some to compass craftily and colours to make;
> And some to ride and recover what unrightfully was won;
> And all He learned to be loyal, and each craft love other.
> Though some be cleaner than some, see ye well, quoth He,
> That he that followeth the fairest craft to the foulest I could
>   have put him;
> Look that none blame other, but love all as brethren;
> And who that most mastery can be mildest of bearing,
> *And crown conscience king and make work* [craft] *your steward.*'

It is in a later canto of the poem, in 'The Vision of Do wel: Do bet: Do best,' that the exaltation of the Plowman takes place, and Christ Himself is represented under the figure of the Peasant, in His suffering and humiliation, as the great Social Emancipator. The Poet represents himself as falling asleep in church during the celebration of the Holy

Mysteries — the Christ Mass — and dreaming this dream of the Christ:

> ' I fell eftsoon to sleep, and suddenly I met
> That Piers the Plowman, was painted all bloody
> And came in with a cross, before the common people,
> And right like in all things to our Lord Jesus.
> And then called I Conscience to ken me the truth.
> Is this Jesus the jouster? quoth I, that Jews did to death?
> Or is it Piers Plowman? who painted him so red?
> Quoth Conscience and kneelèd then, these are Christes arms,
> His colours and coat armour, and he that cometh so bloody
> It is Christ with His Cross, Conqueror of Christendom.
>
> . . . . . .
>
> For our joy and our health Jesus Christ of Heaven,
> In a poor man's apparel pursueth us ever,
> And looketh upon us in their likeness and that with lovely cheer,
> To know us by our kind heart and casting of our eyes
> Whether we love the lords here before our Lord of bliss.
> For all we are Christ's creatures and of His coffers rich,
> And brethren as of one blood, as well beggars as earls.'

Here, then, once more is an answer to my question: 'How do our English poets help us to realise the Personality of Christ?'

This conception of the Peasant-Poet of the Malvern Hills is surely a very noble one! 'Jesus Christ of Heaven in a poor man's apparel pursueth us ever!' Here, it is true, is no figure of a Christ reigning supreme in far-off splendour, in the glory of the Heavenly palaces, or, as in the Christian saga-poem of Cynewulf, leading His thegns and æthelings to battle with the evil legions of the wicked angels and casting them down to doom in Hell, but a figure of the homely and the friendly Christ, dwelling with humble men, helping them with their crafts, teaching them 'to plough and to ditch and to live a leal life and a true'; a Divine Comrade, 'not too bright and good for human nature's daily food'; the great Companion full of love and sympathy for all the sorrows and sufferings of the poor, full of care and concern also for the wider good of the common weal; a Reformer, an Emancipator of the captive and the oppressed, the Champion of social rights, the Inspirer of social duty.

III.—BROWNING.

Lastly, to come to our own day, who is the Poet of keenest spiritual insight who shall interpret for us the Christ of modern theology? To which prophet of the present shall we appeal?—to Wordsworth, to Clough, to Matthew Arnold, to Lowell, to Whittier, to Whitman, to Keble, to Newman, to Sir Edwin Arnold, to Lord Tennyson?

In the poems of all these, no doubt, we shall find many features, scattered lineaments, that may go to make the vision of 'the glory of God shining in the face of Jesus Christ'—the perfect Face. But for to-night, at any rate, I cannot, for myself, ask you to go elsewhere than to the *Christmas Eve* of Robert Browning. Beyond all question, to my mind, Browning is the most deeply religious Poet of our day, perhaps the greatest religious Christian Poet that England has ever had; for this reason if for no other, that he has worked out with splendid subtlety and force, and in every conceivable variety of phase, *the immanence of the Divine in man*, which is the essential truth of the doctrine of the Incarnation.

The poem of *Christmas Eve* is written on the motive which is central to so much of his poetry, that love is the supreme transfiguring power of life, and that, therefore, love is the one thing needful also to true worship, the 'good part,' which, for those who choose it, Christ will not suffer any diversity of creed or development of doctrine ever to take from any one of us. The Poet tells how one Christmas Eve he was driven by stress of weather to take refuge in a little Dissenting chapel, a poor place, standing disconsolate, with a few houses near it, on the edge of a desolate common. The unsavoury atmosphere, 'the hot smell and the human noises,' the unattractive, in some cases repulsive, worshippers—above all,

> 'The preaching man's immense stupidity,
> As he poured his doctrine forth full measure
> To meet his audience's avidity,'

as in fine irreverence he pulled the Book of Books to pieces, and proved to demonstration how the Egyptian

> 'Baker's dream of baskets three
> Proved doctrine of the Trinity'—

all these are too much for the fine sensibilities of the Poet, and he 'flings out of the little chapel' into the wind and rain, in utter disgust at the paltry and narrow faith of these professed worshippers of Christ. He will worship God in the fresh, free air. The open heaven shall be his temple:

> 'When, lo! what think you? suddenly
> The rain and the wind ceased, and the sky
> Received at once the full fruition
> Of the Moon's consummate apparition.
> The black cloud-barricade was riven
> Ruined beneath her feet, and driven
> Deep in the West; while bare and breathless
> North and South and East lay ready
> For a glorious Thing that dauntless, deathless,
> Sprang across them, and stood steady.
> 'Twas a moon rainbow, vast and perfect,
> From heaven to heaven extending, perfect
> As the Mother-moon's self, full in face.
> It rose, distinctly at the base
> With its seven proper colours chorded,
> Which still in the rising were compressed
> Until at last they coalesced,
> And supreme the spectral creature lorded
> In a triumph of whitest white,—
> Above which intervened the night.
> But above night, too, like only the next,

> The second of a wondrous sequence,
> Reaching in rare and rarer frequence,
> Till the heaven of heavens was circumflext,
> Another rainbow rose, a mightier,
> Fainter, flushier, and flightier,—
> Rapture dying along its verge!
> Oh, whose foot shall I see emerge,
> WHOSE, from the straining topmost dark
> On to the keystone of that arc?'

Then follows the vision of the Christ, 'He Himself with His human air,' who had been in the chapel, too, and had left it apparently with the Poet. The disciple tries to justify himself in some sort for despising Christ's friends.

> 'I thought it best that Thou, the Spirit,
> Be worshipped in spirit and in truth,
> And in beauty as even we require it—
> Not in the forms burlesque, uncouth,
> I left but now, as scarcely fitted
> For Thee.   .   ,   .   .   Then
> The whole Face turned upon him full,
> And he spread himself beneath it,
>   .   . saturate with brightness.'

And the Master accepts the love, mistaken and imperfect though it is. He gathers the suppliant, as it were, in the folds of His long, sweeping garment, carries him across the world, and in vision, ' whether in the body or out of the body, he cannot tell,' shows him other sights of other worshippers—at the high festival on Christmas Eve in St. Peter's at Rome, in the Lecture-room of the sceptical Professor at Göttingen—sheep of the Good Shepherd who are not of this fold—and teaches him all the lesson of His Love, until at last the disciple, at the bidding of Love,

> 'From the gift looking to the Giver,
> And from the cistern to the River,
> And from the finite to Infinity,
> And from man's dust to God's Divinity,
>
> . . . . . .
>
> Taking God's help, has attained to think
> Man's heart does best to receive in meekness
> That mode of worship, as most to His mind,
> Where earthly aids being cast behind,
> His All in all appears serene,
> With the thinnest human veil between,
> Letting the Mystic Lamps, the Seven,
> The many motions of His Spirit,
> Pass, as they list, to earth from Heaven.'

My friends, have we attained to this worship of the Christ? or have we indeed any real Christ to worship? Is He real to you? I do not ask you under what aspect you regard Him: whether with Cynewulf and the prophet of old you picture to your soul the Imperial Figure of a King and Conqueror, 'who cometh from Edom, with dyed garments from Bozrah, glorious in apparel, in the greatness of His strength.' I do not ask you whether with the Peasant-Poet of the Middle Age you picture Him as the Social Emancipator, the great Companion of the poor, who in 'all their afflictions was afflicted, and by the angel of His presence'—the presence of a very human and friendly Christ—'saved them.' I do not ask you whether with the modern Poet you picture Him as a mystical Christ, appearing in vision to a poet-soul, and 'yet quick and powerful as any two-edged sword to the piercing asunder' not only of all the formal and conventional orthodoxies of life, but also of all the difficult problems of philosophy and faith. It matters not whether you see the Christ in His lineaments of awe and pity, or of royalty and love, or of everlasting patience and fire-sifting judgment, if He is only a real Christ to you, a burning Image in your heart, illuminating, inspiring, transfiguring life.

To many of you, thank God, in this church tonight I know He is this, your soul's Master and Guide. I know He is more than I, or even any Poet, can express. But if there are those—as, alas! there must be those—in such a congregation as this, who have not yet attained to this fulness of faith, to them I would say, on this Christmas Eve: As surely as in the Christ-child at Bethlehem there lay the power which has run through all the world, so only, if you are sincere, there lies in your desire for Christ enfolded infinite possibilities of growth and power. The

Christhood at present in your hearts may be small. This Christ of yours may be a mere child. But the message of Christmas, if it means anything, means the pledge and promise of infinite possibilities; and the message of Christmas finds its completion in the message of the Ascension. The Son of Man is also the Lord of Glory.

Ah, friends, believe it! The conquering Spirit of Life reigns throughout the world, for Christ has ascended up on high and sat down at the right hand of God.

'The right hand of God!' But where is that?

'*Dextra Dei est ubique!*'

Yes, the old Christian Fathers spoke true: 'The right hand of God is everywhere.' The kingdom of Christ is an everlasting kingdom.

I have read somewhere in a book of Eastern travels that among the Mussulmans of Damascus there is a tradition that as the Ascension of Jesus into Heaven took place on the Mount of Olives at Jerusalem, so His Descent at the Last Day to judge the world will be on the Mountain of Figs at Damascus. In honour of the legend one of the minarets of the great mosque there is called the Minaret of Isa—the Tower of Jesus. And as every prayer offered within those walls is thought by the Mohammedans to be sure of answer, for many a long year they have rigidly excluded every Christian believer from the mosque. But the mosque was once a Christian church—one of the earliest of Christian churches. And above the great entrance gate the followers of Christ who to-day may not cross its threshold may still read the words inscribed there in imperishable mosaic by its Christian builders in the fourth century. They are the words of the 145th Psalm, with the addition of but one word, that of the Holy Name: 'Thy kingdom, O Jesus, is a kingdom for all the ages.'

Yes, my friends, that is the song of praise and triumph which the Church of the Imperial Christ demands from each one of us to-day. 'Thy kingdom, O Christ, is an everlasting kingdom.' We stand, you and I, not outside the gate only, I trust, offering a mere nominal reverence, a mere conventional worship to the Holy Name; we are privileged to enter within the courts of prayer and praise, to join in adoration of the Incarnate Lord, whose kingdom is an everlasting kingdom. 'Regnum tuum, Domine, regnum omnium sæculorum: et dominatio tua in omni generatione et generationem.' Through all the ages and through all the realms Christ claims to be supreme. 'All things that the Father hath are His.' All things —there is no limitation: all History, all Science, all

Poetry, all Art, all Music, all Politics, all Philosophy, all Truth, in whatever realm of human thought or action it may be. Ah, friends, the Christ of Christ's own teaching is a wider Christ than the Christ of our imagining! The Imperial Christ still giveth gifts unto men—apostles, prophets, saints, evangelists, pastors, teachers. He spake by the prophets of old: He speaks by the prophets now: David and Isaiah and Job, Confucius and Buddha and Zoroaster, Pythagoras and Plato, Virgil and Augustine, Hildebrand and Bernard, Cynewulf, and Caedmon, and Langland, Dante and Raphael and Shakespeare, Luther and Beethoven, Descartes and Newton and Darwin, Wordsworth and Emerson and Browning, all heaven and earth are vocal with this imperious song of praise—'Give unto the Christ, O ye sons of the mighty, give unto the Christ glory and strength. Worship the Christ in the beauty of holiness!'

www.ingramcontent.com/pod-product-compliance
Lightning Source LLC
Chambersburg PA
CBHW031812230426
43669CB00009B/1114